M000221556

Lucky You!

Also by Randall Fitzgerald

The Complete Book of Extraterrestrial Encounters

Porkbarrel: The Unexpurgated Grace Commission Story of Congressional Profligacy (with Gerald Lipson)

When Government Goes Private

Cosmic Test Tube: Extraterrestrial Contact, Theories, and Evidence

Mugged by the State

LUCKY YOU!

Proven Strategies You Can Use to Find Your Fortune

Randall Fitzgerald

CITADEL PRESS
Kensington Publishing Corp.
www.kensingtonbooks.com

CITADEL PRESS BOOKS are published by

Kensington Publishing Corp.
850 Third Avenue
New York, NY 10022

All Kensington titles, imprints, and distributed lines are available at special quantity discounts for bulk purchases for sales promotions, premiums, fund-raising, educational, or institutional use. Special book excerpts or customized printings can also be created to fit specific needs. For details, write or phone the office of the Kensington special sales manager: Kensington Publishing Corp., 850 Third Avenue, New York, NY 10022, attn: Special Sales Department; phone: 1-800-221-2647.

First printing: February 2004

10   9   8   7   6   5   4   3   2   1

Printed in the United States of America

Library of Congress Control Number: 2003104690

ISBN 0-8065-2541-X

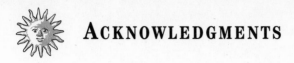

ACKNOWLEDGMENTS

Good fortune blessed me in the form of immensely supportive friends and relatives who provided assistance and encouragement during my five-month frenetic immersion in the research and writing of this book. My parents, Truman and Ruth, my brother Gerald, and my sister Jonna assisted in a variety of loving ways.

Donald Altman gave me wise counsel, as he always does, and Elizabeth Solliday and Megan Anderson provided help at critical moments in the process. I also owe a debt of gratitude to Rollo's, Lake County's premier java house, to its proprietor Rodney Grisso, and to Inna and Kouraleen, who kept me energized with double lattes and stimulating conversation.

My thanks to my agents, Bill Gladstone and Kimberly Valentini of Waterside Productions, and to Michaela Hamilton and Ann LaFarge of Kensington Publishing, for making this book a reality. A special thanks is due to the many dozens of people who consented to be interviewed about their experiences.

Contents

INTRODUCTION

When Fortune Smiles

During my descent into misfortune I often muttered melancholy words of victimhood from an Eric Clapton song—"If it wasn't for bad luck, I wouldn't have no luck at all." The stability and security of both my personal and professional life had simultaneously been shaken by a series of unlucky breaks, cruel twists of fate, and successive failures I seemed powerless to control, all of which I blamed on the vagaries of chance. Feeling abandoned by good fortune, I felt myself surrendering to a pathetic despair. But then something extraordinary and totally unexpected happened. I met a one-armed bandit who changed my life!

From the summer of 2001 into January 2002, my travails included losing a primary source of income when newly installed editors at *Reader's Digest,* a magazine for which I had written for two decades, decided to replace me as part of a restructuring. Due to this loss of income, the cost of an emergency roof replacement on my house that insurance wouldn't cover, and the burden of other accumulated debts, I was forced to file Chapter 13 bankruptcy. My wife of just a few months' duration chose this period to declare that she had never really loved me. She then left me for another man and I filed for divorce. To pay taxes and debts, and just to survive, since I had been unable to find other employment, I had to put my house up for sale. But after five months it had failed to attract a single reasonable offer. By February my entire financial well-being amounted to just $1,200, and I was beginning to have anxiety attacks over how I would pay that month's mortgage and other bills. For the first time in my fifty years, a convergence had occurred between feelings of helplessness and hopelessness.

On the afternoon of February 2, I drove past the Konocti Vista Casino on Clear Lake, one of three casinos in California's Lake County operated by separate bands of Pomo Indians. On impulse I decided to stop in and pay my respects. Just inside the entrance to the tentlike structure a banner greeted me: "Loosest Slots in the State." At the time I had no idea what "loose" meant when applied to a slot machine. I had never really gambled before, except briefly on three occasions when business trips had taken me to Atlantic City and Las Vegas. But the word "loose" seemed significant since, in my luckless and dejected state of mind, any edge, even an illusory one, that promised to defy coldhearted chance, sounded too appealing to ignore.

Within a minute or two of being inside the noisy, smoky casino, I found myself standing in front of a bank of dollar slot machines, eight of them, situated next to a cashier's window. An elderly woman had just won several hundred dollars in one of the machines. She peered over at me through thick glasses, her pale blue eyes sparkling with excitement, and laying her hand lightly on the machine as if it were an old friend, softly proclaimed, "This one has been good to me." After a quick tour of the casino I walked back to that machine, now unattended, sat down on a stool in front of it, and inserted a twenty-dollar bill. I made the maximum bet, two dollars, and began pressing the "Play" button. After several presses I began to win small amounts, and each time I played back the winnings. A few minutes later I hit a small jackpot of $400. I was pleasantly surprised, but promptly collected my booty and walked out of the casino. It was beginner's luck, I told myself, something that might never happen again.

What occurred the next day is exactly what casinos count on to lure fledgling gamblers back and get them hooked. My curiosity about the prospect of winning again captured my imagination, so I drove back to the casino. I felt detached, calmly intent on watching my own actions and my interactions with the machines as if I were merely an observer. Sitting down in front of the same machine I had won on the day before—Numero Uno, I named it—I once again fed it a twenty-dollar bill. A few minutes later I won a $320 payout. I walked out with my winnings, feeling triumphant.

You can imagine what happened next because it's probably a typical scenario confessed at Gamblers Anonymous meetings. I had become fascinated with this machine and curious about how long I could surf this wave of luck. Except for perusing the Help Wanted ads and writing proposals for freelance magazine articles, I had considerable time on my hands. So, on February 6, a Wednesday afternoon, I was back in front of Numero Uno, feeding it twenty-dollar bills. This time I didn't seem to be winning anything at all. I fed it several more twenties. Suddenly, a red seven followed by two blackjack symbols, each a multiplier of the seven's value, fell into place on the payline. A light atop the machine began flashing for an attendant. I had won $2,400, and I was absolutely thrilled.

It seemed as if fortune had begun to smile on me. Now I could actually pay my mortgage and all the other bills due that month, and breathe just a little easier. Okay, I told myself, you got lucky in finding a "loose" machine in a casino that advertises itself as having loose slots. This must be the simple explanation for my run of luck. Yet, an intuitive voice spoke up, overruling my rational mind, not with words but with a feeling that something important had manifested for me to explore.

This first big jackpot marked the beginning of an intriguing and quite lucrative experiment, a conscious decision on my part to challenge chance, and in so doing document my findings and eventually combine what I learned with the secrets of other lucky people. Two friends, Donald Altman and Elizabeth Solliday, both trained as psychologists, became my witnesses and confidants in this experiment. Almost daily I kept them informed in detail of my activities, my intuitive states of mind, and the synchronicities, those meaningful patterns of coincidence, that became the sign-posts I used to help navigate this curious and remarkable path.

The Luck Streak Intensifies

About mid-afternoon on Wednesday, February 27, I suddenly had a "vision" and an irresistible urge to play one of the dollar slot machines (not Numero Uno) on which I had seen a man hit three white sevens for $450 just days earlier. The image of this particular machine and its three white sevens floating into view was so compelling, the electric sensation of a certain destiny so possessed me, that logical and prudent behavior no longer seemed an option. I leapt up and grabbed my car keys.

During my thirty-minute drive to the casino, that image of those three white sevens kept recurring. On arriving, I marched through the casino and straight up to the machine featured in my "vision," and fed it a twenty-dollar bill. The first two button pushes of three dollars each yielded nothing on the payline. On the third push I watched, entranced, as three white sevens fell into place and a light atop the machine began flashing for an attendant to pay me the $450 in winnings.

While waiting for a pay attendant, I casually reached over and fed two dollars into Numero Uno, the machine that had launched this odyssey for me. Bing, bing, bing, and three multi-colored sevens immediately popped up, earning me another $80. This definitely doesn't look and feel like an ordinary string of coincidences, I recall thinking. I certainly don't, as a normal rule, experience dreams or "visions" that come true. So how could I rationally account for this unusual sequence of events?

Now $519 better off (after subtracting what I had put into the machines), I left the casino and drove along the shoreline of Clear Lake to the Konocti Spa, where I sometimes exercised. The woman at the spa's front desk handed me a lock to use in the men's dressing room. Out of fifty or more possible lock numbers, the one she chose for me at random was lock number seven! At that moment the synchronistic significance of the recurring number seven jolted me into a realization. Somehow I knew, with unwavering certainty, that seven would be the Mega number drawn later that evening in the California lottery.

Without bothering to exercise, I immediately drove to the closest convenience store selling lottery tickets. I filled out five tickets using seven as the Mega number out of twenty-seven possible Mega numbers. For the other five numbers in each pick, since I had no strong feeling about them, I simply let the computer choose at random. As I handed these tickets over to the store clerk I noticed the time was exactly seven P.M. When the drawing occurred an hour later, the Mega number, as I had predicted, came up seven! Only a couple of the other numbers matched, however, so I won just a small sum. But the accuracy of my prediction about the Mega so elated me that I felt infused with a sense of wonder.

This sort of magical thinking, applied to gambling, can be a dangerous and expensive trap. It is the kind of belief that casinos encourage as part of their psychological campaign to entice people to play back whatever they win based on a delusional expectation of winning more and more. My sister, Jonna, a former marketing executive with Caesar's Palace in Las Vegas, sobered me with her cautionary advice. "The casinos support any ideas or superstitions that will keep people in the casino spending money. That's why there are no clocks or windows in casinos. They work hard to create a timeless and energetic environment with coins hitting trays, flashing lights, bells, whistles, and other sounds, all designed to whip people into a spending frenzy and make them believe that magic and miracles and instant millionaires are being made all around them. The longer you play, the more the odds advantage the casino."

While I knew she was correct, and I appreciated her warning, it also seemed important to continue my experiment. During the entire week leading up to Saturday, March 9, I had been battling the flu and spent a lot of time in bed. On Friday a termite inspection of my house had found that numerous repairs would have to be made before a sale could occur, and I spent a restless night worrying about the ultimate cost of complying with the inspection report. Feeling somewhat better on Saturday morning, I drove—as if on automatic pilot—to the casino, feeling myself drifting into a meditative state, a sensation of being totally in the moment without the usual cacophony of thoughts. Everything, including my own actions, I regarded with calm detachment. I had entered what I can only describe as the "zone."

Choosing a dollar machine I had never played on before, I deposited a one-hundred-dollar bill—proceeds from my previous play—and began pressing the "Three Credits" button. After thirteen pulls and $39 spent, I hadn't won a single dollar back. I stopped playing for a minute and let my mind go blank. Without any thought, no mental calculating at all, just an intuitive sensation of being in "the zone," I visualized two of the ten-times pay symbols and a Mega (jackpot) symbol rolling into view onto the payline. I replayed this image several times in my mind's eye, then pushed the "Play" button. To my rational mind what happened next seemed totally incomprehensible and impossible: I sensed a shift in the alignment of symbols within the slot machine. I know this sounds delusional (as my later investigation into how slot machines operate would seem to confirm), but I actually saw the alignment occur, as above the payline a triple row of triple bars, and below the payline a triple row of sevens came into view. A second push of the "Play" button and once again these same symbols appeared above and below the payline. At this point I had an uncanny sense that something extraordinary was about to happen. A third push of the "Play" button and symbols whirled into a blur on all three cylinders. Then, in quick succession, a ten-times pay symbol fell into place on the payline, followed by a second ten-times pay symbol and a Mega symbol which just missed the third position on the payline and fell directly below it, to be replaced by a double bars symbol. The machine lit up and a message flashed:

"See attendant for 6,000 credits." The double bars were worth sixty dollars, times ten, times ten, for a payout of $6,000! A casino attendant, accompanied by two security guards, counted out sixty $100 bills into my hand.

The next day my real estate agent called to report he had received the cost estimate for house repairs from a termite inspection company. I gasped in astonishment when I heard the estimated figure of $5,550, almost the sum that I had just won. Mere coincidence or not, somehow it seemed as if the Universe was giving me exactly what I needed to survive.

After winning a $1,000 jackpot in a dollar machine at Konocti on March 17—once again, on a machine I had never played before—I decided it was time to bring this experiment to the attention of my literary agent, Bill Gladstone, for consideration of whether a book on luck might be worthwhile.

My four previously published books had been concerned with an eclectic range of subjects, from public policy and government to the search for other life in the universe, so tackling the subject of good luck fell well within my comfort zone. Bill reacted with enthusiasm to the idea; he considers himself a "lucky person" and the topic had always intrigued him. At the end of our conversation he suggested that I broaden my experiment and test my streak of luck at other casinos.

That very afternoon, I drove to the Twin Pines Casino outside Middletown, a twenty-minute drive east of my home. I had never played in this particular Pomo Indian casino, though I had driven by it dozens of times on my way up and over Mt. St. Helena on trips into the Napa Valley and back. For some reason I decided, even before walking in, that I would only play a ten-times dollar machine like the one at Konocti that had generously rewarded me. The only ten-times dollar machine at Twin Pines stood anonymously in the middle of a long bank of dollar machines. I sat down and began playing the maximum bet of three dollars. Five minutes or so passed and I hit a jackpot—triple bars, triple bars, times ten on the payline, for $900! A few days later I went to another Pomo casino in Hopland, west of Clear Lake, and hit $500 on the first pull on the first machine I played. Lady Luck had become my shadow no matter where I stood.

My lucky streak in the casinos lasted eleven weeks (February 2 to April 22), during which time I won twelve jackpots of $400 or more. The streak ended a few days after the sale of my house. It felt to me at the time as if the house sale profits, creating relief from my financial difficulties, somehow, not coincidentally, also signaled the end of my love affair with Lady Luck.

Other unexpected blessings appeared in my life during the months of March and April. After my house sold at the price I had been asking, I quickly found an equally desirable house to rent nearby. A transient I had befriended at a coffee shop, a Vietnam veteran with a generous heart and resources no one suspected, handed me a gift in appreciation of our conversations. I unwrapped the package to find a new gold Omega watch.

A Journey to Find Answers

As I will explain later, the contrast between winning and losing afforded me the opportunity to discover insights about the relationship between intuition, premonitions, synchronicity, and luck streaks. Over time I noticed a pattern that separated slot winning and losing based on my state of mind. When I set an intention or an expectation of winning—in short, got greedy—I always seemed to lose. Similarly, if I forced myself to play while feeling as if I would lose, and if I was compulsive about my play, I always lost. But when I had **no conscious attachment** to the outcome, and especially when I entered the "zone," I usually came out ahead. Could this be a behavioral secret of luck? Might there be a way of entering this "zone" at will? Or was I simply engaging in delusional, superstitious thinking? I set out to explore these questions.

In a real sense our lives resemble those slot machines. Every day we pull the lever of chance on our finances, our health, our safety, and our relationships. To extend the gambling analogy, at birth we are dealt a hand of cards to play. Some people receive a winning hand—born into wealth, blessed with physical or mental resources—yet squander it all through impatience or ineptitude. Others are dealt average or less-than-average hands, yet manage to play their cards with skill and attract their own lucky breaks. As we will investigate in Part Three of this book, lucky people have learned how to create the right balance of attitude, practice, and behavior most conducive to creating opportunities for luck.

Is there a positive and negative energy flow in life, composed of currents that periodically sweep some of us up and callously fling us aside, while other people skillfully circumnavigate the negative and willfully surf the positive? The odds of winning a state lottery have been likened to being struck by lightning. But people do win lotteries and a few have actually won repeatedly, just as people are struck by lightning repeatedly and survive (thus becoming unlucky and lucky at the same time). Good luck and being struck by lightning sometimes seems to run in families, as if some of us possess a genetic predisposition for what we attract. Or, if you believe in karma, we each have a karmic predisposition to attract good or bad fortune. In my own family, both my father and brother have attracted lightning strikes in separate incidents. Both escaped serious injury, though I hasten to add that neither of them has ever won the lottery.

This book isn't just a collection of stories about gambling and gamblers, though it does reveal many of their tips and techniques. Games of chance are treated in these pages as a convenient process, using money as a tool to keep score, a short feedback loop between action and reward that will enable us, in an anecdotal way, to monitor our own experiments into the ebb and flow of our fortunes.

"The perfect place to observe the laws of chance in action is a casino," says Mike Orkin, a professor of statistics at California State University, one of the many experts on chance and luck whose words I will be quoting. "In the carefully controlled confines of the citadels of chance, reverence is paid to randomness through (those) rituals of risk known as gambling games. Games of chance provide metaphors for life's uncertainties."

This book is for anyone who has ever wanted to experiment with ways of attracting more luck into every aspect of life. You will discover how to decipher your intuition, your dreams, and the synchronicities that occur, and how to open doorways to realize your own luck-making opportunities. You will learn the results of scientific experiments documenting the role that clairvoyance, precognition, and other "sixth sense" capacities may play in our ability to anticipate, recognize, or even to influence the occurrence of luck. You will discover the spiritual dimension of good fortune, its principles revealed by lucky people who use a range of practices—meditation, prayer, affirmations, visualizations—to help manifest their dreams of prosperity.

The research and interviews for this book became both a personal quest for insights and answers to questions about the nature of my own streak of luck, and a journey to document the patterns of attitudes and behaviors that distinguish lucky people from those plagued by bad luck. My travels took me to dozens of casinos in three states, where I observed countless slot, card, dice, and roulette players, and analyzed their streaks of luck, both good and not so good. I interviewed scientists on the frontiers of parapsychological research investigating the roles that intuition and premonitions might play in generating or influencing streaks of luck. At each step of the way, I tried to play the role of journalistic witness or observer, a guinea pig in my own experiment.

It is human nature to wonder why some people seem blessed with good luck, while others seem afflicted with misfortune. What exactly is luck? What does being lucky really mean? Can we control the flow of it, or must we resign ourselves to being at its mercy? Is luck only about chance and the law of averages, or could other factors be clandestinely at work in a lucky person's favor? Do we have access to some innate capacity to create our own reality? Is getting into fortune's energetic flow—and staying there—a skill we can learn? What are "hunches" and how can we harness this force of human nature? What attitudes, perspectives, and practices can increase our opportunities for success? If luck is a gift, must we reciprocate its blessings, or somehow invest in it, to assure that it isn't taken away from us? What *is* the spiritual dimension of good fortune, and how can we use it to enhance our everyday lives? These were among the questions motivating my search for the footprints of Lady Luck's passage.

You have probably heard the expression "Happiness is a journey and not a destination." So it is with luck. Most of us borrow luck, but few of us own it. Some of those who do seem to have ownership rights will have much to teach us in the following pages. So I ask that you suspend disbelief, put aside judgment, forget your preexisting notions of what luck should look and feel like, and come on this journey with me to discover the secrets of lucky people.

PART ONE

EVEN BAD LUCK
CAN DEFY THE ODDS

CHAPTER 1

An Energetic Force Shadowing Us

"Luck affects everything."—*Ovid, first century A.D.*

If you are reading these words, you are a product of chance and luck. You've already won a lottery, overcoming odds of 100 million to one. That's about how many sperm cells your father produced at one time, each representing different genetic traits, and each engaged in a race to fertilize your mother's egg. One of them prevailed, resulting in you. Congratulations on winning the "womb lottery." All of us are, quite literally, lucky to be alive.

We live in a world where chance is a normal part of everyday life. Unforeseen and surprising events have always affected humankind, for better and for worse, and we remain forever at the mercy of luck to some extent, no matter how diligently we may prepare, or how cleverly we design strategies to anticipate the unexpected. We owe our entire existence as a species to chance and luck. Humans got very lucky, for instance, when that asteroid hit the planet millions of years ago and wiped out the dinosaurs so mammals could inherit the earth and evolve into us.

Luck, as most of us understand chance occurrence, operates on two levels simultaneously—the macro, and the micro—to impact our lives. In the macro realm, such as natural disasters, we exercise little if any control. Every disaster produces lucky survivors and unlucky victims. People lose homes or their lives in tornadoes and earthquakes, and others escape unscathed. During the collapse of the World Trade Center towers some people perished, while others escaped. Disease epidemics used to be the great equalizer of the macro realm, historically tending to determine the lucky and the unlucky with a swift and fierce randomness.

Being at the wrong place at the right time gave us the expression "There but for the grace of God go I." In the micro realm of our personal actions, as we will explore in Parts Two and Three of this book, we may sometimes influence outcomes either directly, or in subtle ways at the margins. Our intuition, if harnessed and properly interpreted, may sometimes help us to avoid calamities, or may lead us with unswerving confidence toward luck-generating opportunities.

"Luck prevents life from being too rational and too predictable," observes Nicholas Rescher, a professor of philosophy at the University of Pittsburgh. "Luck is a great populist force that gives everyone a chance. . . . The prospect of luck brings hope to the otherwise hopeless."

Belief Systems Around Luck

Historian Stephen Ambrose once described luck as a sort of lubricant for great historical events. "I firmly believe that history is chance, just like evolution. It's not the survival of the fittest, it's the survival of the luckiest."

Throughout recorded history every culture has developed a belief system describing luck as an energy shadowing us, in both positive and negative ways, to shape individual lives and influence the collective course of human events. Many of the spiritual practices and traditions of world religions have their roots in the earliest recorded examples of human attempts to harness luck. Going back to at least 3200 B.C., Egyptians used beads they called "sha," a word meaning luck, as prayer talismans in religious rituals seeking the blessings of Egyptian gods. These "sha sha" beads, as ancient Egyptians called them, were worn with the intent of giving the wearer the energy of good fortune.

In India, Hindus adopted the use of bead strands called "malas," a Sanskrit word for "rose" or "garland," consisting of 108 beads, for repeating mantras or counting their breaths in meditation. Around 500 B.C., according to religious historians, the new religion of Buddhism also embraced the use of malas for mantras and meditations. Roman Catholicism continued this tradition in the form of the Catholic rosary, which comes from the word rosarium, meaning "rose garden." Muslims use prayer beads, as do many Native American tribes and African tribes such as the Yoruba in Nigeria, whose beads represent the qualities of spiritual wisdom.

For people of the ancient world, this powerful force called luck was embodied as a god and worshipped in order to attract its blessings. Dynastic Egypt had the good luck deities of Bes and Beset, the classical Greeks had Hermes, and Romans prayed to the goddess Fortuna. She was depicted on Roman coins holding both a cornucopia, symbolizing prosperity, and a rudder to identify her as the controller of destinies. In the Roman temples dedicated to venerating Fortuna, priestesses operated oracles for visitors with responses based on the outcomes of die-tosses, thus adding chance—and even gambling—to the process of fortune telling. Fortuna, the goddess, eventually became that capricious mistress known to us today as Lady Luck.

Ancient peoples evolved numerous complex rituals and beliefs designed to access, or to foretell, good fortune, and to warn of impending perils. Excavations of Stone Age sites throughout the world have found enormous numbers of dice-shaped bones that archaeologists call "astragalia," objects carved from the ankle bones of sheep and other cloven-footed animals, which were apparently used by our Ice Age ancestors for prophecy or gambling. By 2000 B.C. the Egyptians were using dice carved from bone or ivory for both divination and gambling. The Chinese originated the I Ching, the Vikings used runes, African tribes practiced divination with bones and animal entrails, and other cultures produced astrology, palmistry, numerology, crystal balls, and tarot cards—the origin of playing cards—for gambling.

Around 700 B.C., precognition was a thriving industry in the spiritual life of Greece in the form of predictions made by priest-esses in oracle temples, the most famous being the Oracle of Apollo at Delphi, a village 100 miles from Athens. Historical records pre-serve hundreds of allegedly correct predictions made at Delphi, though, as with many modern seers, no record was kept of incor-rect answers to questions about the future. The most renowned ac-curate prediction from a Delphi priestess to reach us occurred in 480 B.C. when the oracle warned Athenians that a Persian army would burn the city, which did happen, and that an Athenian fleet would then defeat the Persians, which also happened. To celebrate the good fortune of this predicted victory, Athenians built the Parthenon.

The Norman conquest of England in 1066 was memorialized soon thereafter in the Bayeux tapestry with an invasion scene of knights, over whose heads a comet is portrayed as a slash across the sky. Natural portents such as new comets and other celestial phe-nomena, and the earthly events of earthquakes, storms, and the like, were rich with meaning for seers, shamans, and the priestly class, who specialized in linking natural events synchronously with outbreaks of disease, war, and the crowning of kings. In their world-view, affinities and harmonies between people, events, and the natural world periodically merged, creating coincidences they interpreted as harbingers of either good or bad fortune.

The Origins of Our Superstitious Practices

From these early beliefs and ritualistic tools we can trace a wide range of the world's present-day superstitions, a word the Oxford English Dictionary describes as: "the belief in the existence or power of the supernatural; irrational fear of the unknown; a reli-gion or practice based on such tendencies." I must confess that I prefer the definition coined by a former *Time* magazine editor, Max Gunther: "Superstition is any religious, mystical, or occult belief not held by me."

Take the significance of horseshoes. They are considered lucky

talismans because of their open-ended, half-circle shape—a re-
minder of the crescent moon—which is also a design common at
sacred megalithic sites such as Stonehenge in the west of England,
where eclipses and other celestial phenomena were charted and
predicted 4,000 years ago. Similarly, when breaking apart a chicken
wishbone (a ritual dating back to the Etruscans of present-day Italy
in 300 B.C.), whoever ends up with the longest part of the crescent-
shaped bone gets "a lucky break" and can make a wish.

Four-leaf clovers, because they are so rare in nature, became
popular charms in pre-Christian times among Druid priests of the
Celtic tribes who carried them to ward off dark or unlucky forces.
Roman culture devised the amuletum, known today as amulets,
that were worn to protect the wearer against bad luck, whereas
lucky charms, otherwise known as charm bracelets, were for attracting good luck.

Historically, seven has been considered a lucky number, possibly because the ancient Greeks, by combining the four sides of a
square and the three sides in a triangle, thought they had created
the perfect figure. Seven has also been a lucky number in Japanese
culture, dating back to an early folk tale about the Seven Gods of
Luck. The number thirteen, by contrast, seems to have gotten its
unlucky reputation as a result of the Last Supper in Christian tradition, when Christ dined with his twelve disciples, one of whom—
the thirteenth diner—betrayed him.

Consider the origin of some of our most common figures of
speech. "Knock on wood" comes from the Celtic and Teutonic pagan
tribes who engaged in tree worship and thought the act of touching
an enchanted tree could cause tree spirits to grant a lucky wish. Or
take the expression "getting off on the right foot." That dates back
to Roman times, when guards stationed at public buildings en-
forced a law that no one could enter using their left foot first. Why?
Someone in Roman history, probably a priest or an emperor, had
simply decided that placing the left side of the body first was bad
luck. It may also have something to do with the tradition, common
in many cultures, that the right hand is for shaking.

Our wedding rituals are steeped in superstitious beliefs. A bride must cut the wedding cake first for good luck, a practice with an unknown ancient origin. Dating from Roman times, rice is thrown at both bride and groom for good luck in conceiving children. A groom carries his bride over the honeymoon threshold so evil spirits cannot trip her, an old Teutonic custom.

In the English language the very conception of human happiness is intertwined with the idea of luck. The English word "happy" comes from an Icelandic word, "happ," meaning chance or luck, while the word "luck" originates from a fifteenth-century German word, "gluck," meaning both good fortune and happiness.

Superstitions prevalent in Ireland and among the Irish embody one of the more extreme cultural examples of lives being tailored to appease a belief in the energetic forces of good and bad luck. Maybe it is the sheer number of luck-related practices, and the intensity of the belief in them, that spawned that popular term "the luck of the Irish." My friend Brian O'Mahony, the co-owner of a highly successful electrical engineering company, grew up in County Cork, Ireland, about six miles from the fabled Blarney Castle. Like many of his countrymen, Brian is a gifted storyteller, so it seems appropriate to let him describe in his own words the flavor and depth of the Irish attachment to talismans and omens.

"The Blarney stone is a perfect example of what people have done for hundreds of years to attract luck. Someone suspends himself upside down from the top of a medieval castle, hanging down backward in a dangerous and uncomfortable position, to kiss the opposite side of the shaft while being held by his legs. The entire wall of the shaft shines from the erosion of millions of lips being placed on it. This act of kissing is supposed to give you the gift of speech and communication, but it's also associated with good luck. After kissing the Blarney stone, people seem to leave with a boundless optimism about what will happen next in their lives. By living nearby, it felt like we were already grandfathered in, so I never felt it necessary to kiss it myself.

"My life was surrounded with examples of what you did and didn't do for good luck. The Irish countryside is dotted with mounds about fifty yards in diameter that form the exterior wall of ancient

Druidic settlements. They're called fairy forts. To this day I have never met an Irish person who has gone inside the perimeter of a fairy fort. You're told as a child never to go in or something very bad will happen. Farmers always plow their fields around the fort's perimeter. The Irish countryside is dotted with wishing wells, little springs you find in a field and hidden in bushes. When the Irish wanted good luck they would go to these wishing wells and drop an offering of flowers and coins into the water.

"In my family there were numerous rituals we learned from my mother, who spoke Gaelic and was from rural Ireland. When something happens there is always a reason for it, and she would follow a particular ritual to turn the event into something good. Whenever anyone dropped a knife in our kitchen, that meant that a guest would arrive and you had to go to the window or it was bad luck. They call these behaviors superstitions. But there were profound reasons for them. Traditional societies are very much in touch with the psycho-physical nature of reality and take into account all kinds of invisible forces so their lives will be in balance. Bad luck would come if you violated those practices. The fact that some people believe that lucky talismans and behaviors work produces a certainty and confidence in them, and that often seems, in my experience, to create the process where luck can occur."

Luck's Meaning Is Personal

In our present day, perhaps because our desire to clearly delineate everything makes life seem more complicated, even the word "luck" is no longer a simple and direct reference point. Consulting three current dictionaries from various publishers, I found luck defined three slightly different ways, each implying a particular perspective on life. Luck is "that which happens by chance," read one source. Luck is "the force that seems to operate for good or ill in a person's life," declared the second. Luck is "an unpredictable and uncontrollable force that shapes events," offered the third.

Even the mental health field has gotten involved in defining what luck should mean by using the terms "internal" and "external" when referring to locus of control. "Internal locus of control" means a person believes he or she can, through force of will, create lucky events, or at least the opportunities for luck. "External locus of control" refers to people who believe that luck is a force existing outside of them and mostly beyond their control, as in being born under a "lucky star." In this book, case studies will illustrate both definitions, and others beside, because my chief concern is whether the strategies seem to work in practice, not whether one definition is more accurate than another.

No one is in total control of his life and thus immune to the unexpected, so everyone's life is subject to the influence of luck. As a result, no matter what the dictionaries or the experts may tell us we should believe about luck, our personal definition always seems to remain dependent on what our lives have been like.

Our Natural Desire to Find Meaning

Mathematician and probability theorist Dr. Horace Levinson once wrote that only superstitious people can believe they are "haunted by a spirit named luck." Such superstitions, Levinson argued in his book, *Chance, Luck and Statistics*, have roots "in egocentric thinking, in the individual's desire to regard himself as an important part of the scheme of things."

While I can't disagree with Levinson's interpretation, as far as it goes, there is an important element missing that has to do with the extent to which we human beings have a need programmed into us by evolution to attach meaning, not only to the events in our individual lives, but to life in general. Many people believe that the existence of intelligent life, of consciousness itself, has an innate meaning and is the intended product of intelligent design. Other people contend, in the name of rationality, that life is nothing more than a byproduct of chance, and the only meaning to be attached is that concocted by our own egocentric point of view. Either God, an intelligently directed design, does exist, or God does not exist except as a concept invented and nurtured by the human imagination. Which side of the argument you come down on largely shapes your view of whether luck, coincidence, intuition, parapsychology, and spirituality can be objectively validated with meaning.

Nearly all of us harbor a fear, if not a healthy respect, for luck and its unpredictable effects as evidenced by many of our normal conversational habits. We commonly say things to each other like "best of luck" . . . "good luck to you" . . . "tough luck" . . . "better luck next time" . . . "some people have all the luck" . . . "don't push your luck" . . . "your luck is bound to change" . . . "that was a lucky (or unlucky) break" . . . "lucky you!"

Rational, intelligent, and scientific-minded people are no less susceptible to superstitions, or to the idea that luck can be attracted, than the rest of us. The billionaire John D. Rockefeller always carried his lucky stone and rubbed it when making business decisions. British Prime Minister Winston Churchill never went outside for a walk, especially during World War II, without carrying his lucky walking stick. President Franklin Roosevelt was said to have had a morbid fear of the number thirteen, insisting, for example, that his secretary always be available for dinner parties so, in case thirteen people sat down, she could become the fourteenth at the table.

Lucky charms in the form of "fairy cross" stones from southwestern Virginia were carried by U.S. presidents Theodore Roosevelt and Woodrow Wilson, the inventor Thomas Edison, and the famous pilot, Charles Lindbergh, who was nicknamed "Lucky Lindy." American Admiral George Dewey directed the battle of Manila Bay in the Spanish-American War while wearing his lucky rabbit's foot. Nobel Prize-winning physicist Niels Bohr kept a rabbit's foot in his laboratory, and when questioned about it, professed: "I'm told it brings luck whether one believes in it or not."

Behavioral psychologists say that human beings, in our attraction to superstitious practices, resemble pigeons and other species of animals used in lab experiments. In one classic demonstration, B.F. Skinner, a leading behaviorist, fed a group of caged pigeons at regular intervals and noted how they seemed to believe they had control. Whatever pecking, head-bobbing, or other behavior they had been engaged in prior to feeding, it soon became their individual ritual, as if their particular body movements and sounds could willfully and magically create the reward of a feeding experience.

This logical fallacy motivates all human rituals of superstition, so the behaviorist argument goes, and few among us are completely immune. At the beginning of my eleven-week winning streak at slots, for instance, I realized that I had been wearing either green pants or a green shirt the first three times I won, and I was sorely tempted to continue wearing that color each time I gambled. But my rational mind prevailed, at least in this regard, as I understood it would be a mistake to confuse superstition with luck, or to think using a good luck charm is anything more than begging a favor from chance. As if to confirm this view, I continued winning without wearing green garments.

Since in behaviorist theory rewards and consequences help shape behavior, consider what if, just for the sake of argument, I had continued winning slot jackpots every time I wore green, and had lost money every time I failed to wear that color. Over time I certainly would have conditioned myself to suspect that green was somehow connected to my good fortune. If I had gotten carried away in this irrational exuberance, I might even have jumped to the conclusion that since my ancestry is part Irish, and green is generally associated with the so-called "luck of the Irish," I was being rewarded in some karmic way.

Yet, while I find myself agreeing in principle that superstitions are irrational, that we are often silly when we use them, that we may even endanger ourselves and others if we trust too fully or frequently in them, I can't help but wonder if these luck-seeking rituals are symbolic of a fundamental human need and longing that we would be foolish to totally repress and ignore.

A columnist for Beliefnet, a religious and spiritual Internet Web site, similarly wondered what all the fuss is about. "An ounce of superstition may be a good thing," wrote John D. Spalding. "To allow yourself an ounce of superstition is to admit you don't have all the answers. Nature certainly has laws and reason may be humanity's saving grace, but life doesn't follow neat patterns discernible either in a crystal ball or under a microscope. . . . Life is erratic, and it's best lived not as a science, but as an art. . . . Rubbing worry beads or patting a Buddha's belly won't solve your problems, but it might clear your head so *you* can."

We see evidence of this phenomenon in those professions where superstitions seem most connected to reinforcing a mental attitude to enhance performance. Sometimes the feeling of "luck is on my side" does work to one's advantage. Many sports legends have had a fondness for lucky charms and superstitious practices. Basketball star Michael Jordan spent his professional career wearing the shorts from college that he believed had been lucky for him. Hockey star Wayne Gretzky always kept one side of his jersey hanging loose in games. Tennis star Bjorn Borg stopped shaving his face four days before every tournament. Both baseball star Wade Boggs and track star Jackie Joyner-Kersee engaged in a ritual of eating specially pre-pared chicken before a game or track event. Boggs had this to say about his practice: "Superstitions may not be logical or account for what happens on the field. They're routines and rituals for the soul and spirit. They're part of your mental preparation for a game."

Powers of Belief and the Creation of Luck

A belief that luck can be transmitted as energy shows up in many of our modern customs. Garters are still given to brides based on the ancient idea that this item of clothing could pass the luck of a happy marriage from one woman to the next. Shakespeare wrote about luck as "a tide in the affairs of men, which, taken at the flood, leads on to fortune." African-American culture typically uses the word "mojo" to describe that energetic force, a term Robert Johnson made famous in his 1937 recording of the blues song, "Little Queen of Spades," about a gambling woman whose mojo brings large winnings in card games.

As a group, gamblers are probably the most superstitious people on the planet. Watch players at a craps table. Many blow on their dice before throwing them, a vestige of the belief that one can blow life into an inanimate object so it will obey the gambler's bidding. Watch players at a card table or at the roulette wheel. Many will reflexively touch anything or anyone just involved in a lucky payoff, as if from a belief that luck, like an electrical charge, is an energy that can be conducted directly into them.

For one lucky state lottery jackpot winner, luck literally did seem to rub off. After Ed Gildein won $8.9 million in the Texas lottery in 1993, his friend, Irene Scott, would rub his back every time she saw him and say, "I need some luck." Less than two years later, that practice seemed to pay off for Irene. She won a $2.2 million jackpot in the Texas lottery.

This theme of luck as an energetic force helped shape the plot of a critically acclaimed Spanish film, *Intacto*, released in 2002, and starring the Swedish actor Max von Sydow. In it a group of people in the Canary Islands who have the gift of luck play dangerous games of chance organized by a casino owner, played by von Sydow, whose character is a Holocaust survivor. He wraps his arms around one lucky man in a hug that literally steals the man's gift of luck away. Writer and director Juan Carlos Fresnadillo says he got the idea for this film as a young boy after witnessing the aftermath of a deadly collision of two jumbo jets, a shocking experience that inspired him to ponder the unpredictable nature of fate and luck.

Superstitious practices give us a means of asserting some semblance of predictable control and order in our lives, as illusory as that might sometimes be in reality, in the hope that life's uncertainties won't plunge us into a state of psychological chaos. Dr. Edmund Kern, a history professor who has written books on the irrationality of superstition, actually practices a number of superstitions himself as a reality check. "I read my horoscope," he was quoted on the Beliefnet Web site. "I knock on wood religiously. I also do Tarot readings. But I engage in these activities as someone who perceives himself as a rationalist. I don't believe the cards are going to tell me my future, but I do believe that I can learn quite a bit about my feelings and myself by measuring my reactions to the readings."

Former *Time* magazine editor Max Gunther, author of a book called *The Luck Factor*, advises us to "think of a superstition simply as a neat psychological device that can come to your aid in moments of worry, confusion, and indecision. In a situation where you must make a choice but are intimidated by the shortage of facts, a good, friendly superstition helps you avoid paralysis."

Can a belief in superstition, in the power of luck and lucky charms, or conversely in the power of unlucky numbers and the like to affect us negatively, help create a vibratory level of consciousness that attracts what we desire or repels what we fear? Such a question will, by its very nature, cause the eyebrows of an ultra-rationalist to arch and his or her lip to curl, since it implies a heresy for traditional science—that our thoughts can influence the world around us without normal resort to the laws of cause and effect.

Back in 1982 an odd story came to my attention, one that would seem to add anecdotal evidence to this idea that patterns of belief can have consequences in the material realm of our consensus reality. The police department in the West Texas town of Pampa had a fleet of patrol cars that included car number 13, a vehicle some police officers expressed a reluctance to drive because of their superstitious fears that 13 might be unlucky. As if in response to these attitudes, Patrol Car D-13 became accident-prone. "That car kept getting hit," reported Police Chief J. J. Ryzman. "One time an officer was out directing traffic and a car came out of nowhere and hit it. Another time we had it down at the city garage and a dump truck backed into it." As the accidents kept happening to Car 13, police officers labeled this Chevrolet Impala a jinx, and most tried with grim determination to avoid contact with it.

But like one of those possessed vehicles out of a Stephen King novel, Car 13 had seemingly become willful and malicious in its actions. It kept attracting collisions and spent more time in the repair shop than on the city streets. Finally, his department overwhelmed by the repair bills, Chief Ryzman had the car's number changed from D-13 to D-25 in the hope that its luck might be changed. Six months later, the chief told city councilmen how "we haven't had any problem with that vehicle since the changes. It was just a matter of eliminating that number, just like some hotels skip the thirteenth floor."

What are the odds that, out of dozens of police vehicles in that town, the one most associated with what officers believed to be an "unlucky" number would become the most "unlucky" car? Did the collective unconscious of police minds unintentionally create these accident situations? Can our persistent negative thoughts have real, unintended, bad-luck-generating consequences? Such considerations lead us directly into the twilight zone of probability theory, under whose laws almost anything can and will happen.

CHAPTER 2

The Limits of Probability Theory

"Probability is the very guide of life."
—Bishop Butler (1692–1752)

"Fortune and misfortune are like the twisted strands of a rope."—old Japanese saying

What initially intrigued me most about the slot player I named "The Shaman" was the manic energy radiating from his mud-brown eyes. When he appeared inside the Konocti Vista Casino one boiling August afternoon, trailed by a woman companion half his age but twice his size, other slot players stopped feeding their machines long enough to steal startled glances at his soiled and tattered clothes, his emaciated and tattooed body, and the scraggly, gray beard that brushed his chest and which, I kid you not, was streaked with dried mustard, ketchup, and other vestiges of fine dining. Several of the security guards eyed him warily from a respectful distance, as if fearing that he might start frothing at the mouth and gibbering about conspiracies involving space aliens.

At first The Shaman seemed to be scouting out the machines, walking languidly among them, his skinny arms outstretched like a human dowsing rod trying to sense a vein of gold. His eyes were unblinking and intense, but his gaze seemed unfocused, as in a trance. His thirty-something companion, who must have weighed 300 pounds, smiled as she followed several steps behind him, an empty plastic coin bucket squeezed under each of her python-sized arms.

Apparently sensing something, The Shaman planted his boots in front of a quarter machine, one of those Sizzling Seven bandits with a 1,000-coin maximum payout, and fed it a five-dollar bill. As he jabbed the "Play" button with his right index finger, betting three quarters at a time, his left arm jerked spasmodically and flailed the air at shoulder level, as if that side of his body was being periodically convulsed with an epileptic seizure. He reminded me of Joe Cocker, the rock singer featured at Woodstock who twitched and jerked one arm around in exactly the same manner while performing on stage.

Almost immediately, The Shaman began winning ten, twenty, forty coins on practically every push of the "Play" button. Then he hit three sevens worth 300 quarters and cashed out. Quarters cascaded into the metal tray, and The Shaman moved over to stand in front of an adjoining machine as his companion swooped in and began scooping handfuls of the coins into one of her white plastic buckets. No words or even looks were exchanged between these two, prompting me to wonder if over time they had developed some sort of system and routine.

His good-luck streak continued on this second quarter machine. I watched from ten feet away as The Shaman won twenty, thirty, forty quarters on every second or third push of the "Play" button. His pupils appeared to be faintly glowing from the intensity of his focus. He kept punching the "Play" button faster, as fast as the machine would respond, his left arm all the while gyrating and flailing as if he were conducting an invisible orchestra. Within ten minutes his winnings had reached 700 coins. Once again, he hit the "Payout" button, a stream of quarters cascaded, and he moved on as his partner swooped in and began filling the second bucket.

Stakes were higher now because he had migrated across the aisle into a bank of dollar machines, the first being a Blazing Sevens with a three-dollar maximum bet. He played the maximum and started hitting again, a rising crescendo of hits, culminating in three red sevens worth $300. Several envious gamblers from the nearby snack bar were now staring at him, all of them mesmerized, as I was, by the spectacle of this wild, disheveled man so thoroughly immersed in "the zone." (Veteran gamblers call such lucky streaks a "run.")

Wondering if a residual effect existed, a winning backwash inside the slot "consciousness" that I could capitalize on, I sat down at the first machine he had played. Feeling rather like a pilot fish following a slot shark, I started betting three quarters at a time. After pumping in eighty coins I had won exactly two cherries worth three quarters each. I moved on to the second machine he had played. Punch, punch, spin, spin, and soon another eighty quarters had been digested, yielding nothing for me in return. As I would later learn, what often separates slot winners from losers is a millisecond of difference in the timing of their play. I must have been a nearsighted Little Leaguer at bat on this day and The Shaman was a major league home-run hitter.

Meanwhile, The Shaman had filled a bucket to the brim with dollar winnings—his companion had toddled off to a cashier's window to cash in the two buckets of quarters—and he shifted his attention to another Blazing Seven's dollar machine opposite the one he had been playing. He planted himself before it and the ritual commenced. This fourth machine contained the mother lode. In quick succession he hit multa-sevens for $200, then a few strokes later another $200, and finally three red sevens for $300, his spastic left arm always shaking, rattling, and rolling. My lower jaw must have come unhinged because I could no longer contain my awe and amazement at this remarkable spree.

Only when this slot machine's credit counter reached $1,600, which seemed to be a significant number for him, did The Shaman press the "Payout" button, sending a light atop the machine into flash mode. Even as he waited for an attendant to hand-pay his winnings, The Shaman continued playing on an adjoining dollar machine, racking up still more credits. Not long afterward he left the casino, shadowed by his mute companion, both clutching snack bar hamburgers in one hand and thick wads of cash in the other. He became, in my imagination, a shaman, a modern-day Druid of Celtic lore, who had ventured forth from his oak forest lair to conjure up survival funds.

Being a witness to such a feat had felt magical, much like my own eleven-week streak of good luck at slots a few months earlier. During the summer of 2002, as Konocti Vista Casino became a sort of laboratory for me, and I played the role of observing other slot-players and my own slot-playing, making note of our respective monetary ebbs and flows, those memorable streaks of luck such as that which The Shaman exhibited became surprisingly routine.

Sometimes luck seemed to resemble an energetic force sweeping through an entire group of people, a virus spontaneously infecting everyone playing at a bank of machines. One evening I watched a family—a husband and wife in their early thirties, and the wife's parents—sit down at a bank of four adjoining dollar machines, all of which I had just played and had abandoned after nonstop losses. Almost immediately the younger woman, let's call her Marie, won big, hitting a seven and two ten-times pay symbols for a $10,000 jackpot. Marie shrieked with joy and stomped her feet, and her husband and parents joined in for a lively celebratory dance in the aisle. After an attendant counted out a hundred one-hundred-dollar bills into her hands, Marie casually handed several to her husband and several more to her parents and encouraged them all to sit back down and continue playing.

What happened next I can only describe as akin to popcorn in a microwave, one kernel after another zapped into a popping chain reaction. Marie's mother hit for $3,000, sending her machine into a spasm of attention-grabbing noises, and seconds later Marie's father hit a series of mini-jackpots of $100 followed by $200. With each hit the intensity flowing among these four people, which literally felt electrical to those of us observing, was amped up higher as they kept shouting at each other and punching the "Play" buttons faster and faster in a frenzy of motion and emotion. Marie's husband hit three white sevens for $450 on his machine, and when I leaned down and offered my congratulations, the smile vanished from his weather-beaten face. "It ain't nothing," he declared. "You should've seen us the other night."

Admittedly, I was quite charmed to be a witness to these displays of Lady Luck's affections. But should we really be amazed by

these intense individual and group experiences?
statisticians, and scientific materialists insist that
the least bit surprised. In their view, the laws of probabil
with unwavering certainty that both the streaks of good luck a
bad luck in our lives are simply flipsides of the same phenomenon
of defying the odds. All luck is thus reduced to chance occurrence,
and streaks of luck are nothing more than a predicted, periodic
"clustering" of events over time.

Predictable Workings of Chance

After the fall of the Roman Empire a Christian compromise
emerged, maintaining the lingering belief that the Roman goddess
Fortuna influenced our fortunes. That unifying idea, as described
by David and Sharon Hoffman in *Parabola* magazine, was "that
even chance is bound by some law—that with planning and calcu-
lation she can be mastered."

The actual link between gambling and mathematics was made
in the eighteenth century, as this idea called "probability theory"
surfaced from a Frenchman's statistical attempts to provide gamblers with rational guidance on the odds of dice falling a particular
way. Probability theory, write the Hoffmans, "was an attempt to
build mathematical 'dikes and dams' against fortune. But although
the statistics of probability are a valuable tool in large-scale planning, by their nature they tell us little about individual events."

If we are all the result of "a cosmic grand plan that determines
reality," says Mike Orkin, a professor of statistics and author of
What Are The Odds?, "chance is a key tool for implementing that
plan. . . . Playing a slot machine or buying a lottery ticket is a symbolic way of handing your destiny to the fates. Understanding the
laws of chance can help you decide if some ways of handing your
destiny to the fates are better than others."

In its simplest form, probability theory can be described as the
chance expectation, the odds, that any given event will occur. Take
coin flips and the odds of heads or tails turning up. In the short

un, heads or tails may turn up in clusters of, say, four heads followed by eight tails in a row. But over a longer series of flips (100 or more), probability theory predicts the average number of heads or tails appearing will always gravitate to a mean of fifty percent, or very close to it.

How likely is it that someone flipping a coin 100 times will get lucky and flip 100 heads or 100 tails in a row? The odds against chance, as calculated by statistics expert Orkin, amount to a 1 followed by 30 zeros. "If every person on earth, six billion people, starts tossing coins twenty-four hours per day, with each person tossing at the rate of one hundred tosses every five minutes, it will take an average of about a million-billion years until somebody gets one hundred heads in one hundred tosses." That pretty much means it's impossible.

However, to qualify as lucky, you really only have to beat the odds which hold that 100 coin tosses will yield somewhere between 40 and 60 heads. If you consistently toss more than 60 heads out of every 100 flips, especially if heads is the desired result with a reward attached, then you are not only defying chance odds, you are demonstrating "paranormal" luck. For statisticians, as well as for parapsychological scientists, if you consistently toss *fewer* than 40 heads out of every 100 flips—having declared your intention to toss a high number of heads—the fact that you are failing, and defying chance expectation as a consistently big loser, is also a significant aberration. A parapsychologist would say you are exhibiting paranormal bad luck.

For another variation on coin flipping, suppose that 1,000 stock market analysts each flip a coin to determine their prediction of whether the market at year's end will be up or down. Suppose they make these predictions for ten years. Over that decade at least one of the analysts will correctly choose ten out of ten outcomes, if we accept the law of large numbers (that odd things happen by chance given a sufficient number of opportunities.) This one lucky analyst becomes, in the public imagination, a bona fide Wall Street stock-picker guru.

To calculate the odds when five coins at a time are thrown, six dice are rolled, or multiple hands of poker are dealt, rather complex mathematical formulas have been devised. One formula, for instance, reveals the odds that any two people in a room will have the same birthday (as in day and month, not year). Put any ten persons together in the same room and the chances are one in nine that at least two will have the same birthday. Put twenty-three persons together and the odds increase to better than fifty percent, making the "coincidence" of duplicate birthdays almost a probability. With one hundred persons, according to mathematician Warren Weaver, "the odds are better than three million to one that at least two have the same birthday."

To demonstrate the predictable workings of chance, Weaver, then a professor of mathematics at the University of Wisconsin, once collected the yearly statistics for dog bites in New York City. In 1955, on average, 75.3 reports were recorded each day of dogs biting people. In 1956, daily dog bites averaged 73.6 reports. In 1957, the average was 73.2 reports, and so on with little deviation through the ensuing years. British philosopher and novelist Arthur Koestler, on reading these statistics, wryly raised the obvious question: "How do the dogs in New York know that their daily ration of biting is exhausted?" (Were the dogs communicating by ESP? a mischievous mind might inquire.)

Under the laws of probability, just about anything can happen, and if it can happen, it eventually will happen. As Martin Gardner has declared in his various writings on mathematical subjects, "Trillions of events, large and trivial, happen to billions of humans every day. In this vast, turbulent sea of endless happenings, it would be astonishing if coincidences didn't occur."

Randomness proponents often make this point in connection with the game of bridge, in which 635 billion possible hands could be dealt using a deck of cards. There are eight perfect hands that can be dealt in this game. These eight perfect hands, out of 635 billion possible hand combinations, will be dealt once in every 79 billion hands, according to statistical probability. By estimating the number of games of bridge played in the average year, and the number of hands dealt per game, a perfect hand should come into a player's possession somewhere in the United States every three years or so.

"Strange things are predicted by the laws of chance," wrote mathematician Horace C. Levinson, in *Chance, Luck and Statistics*. "Freak runs of luck and striking coincidences . . . the laws of chance are indifferent to the name of the winner."

Gambling casinos owe their considerable earnings to these predictable workings of chance. If probability theory couldn't predict the movements of large numbers, no casino could afford to remain in business. Greg Sexton, the general manager of Konocti Vista Casino, where I did much of my research, typifies the viewpoint of gaming executives. After twenty-five years in gaming, mostly in Las Vegas and Reno, Sexton has seen people experience luck streaks that lasted up to a year. "You're bound to get lucky sometimes. Slot machines will get hot and go through cycles. If you're lucky at picking that machine, you'll beat the odds. But the law of averages will catch up to you eventually. I don't know anybody who consistently beats the odds, or consistently knows how to pick a hot machine, or knows consistently when to quit playing."

After reading the works of mathematicians and randomness theoreticians like Levinson and Warren Weaver, and listening to Sexton and other casino executives, I cannot rationally doubt their basic premise—that over long enough periods of time, random events can conspire to produce patterns of lucky breaks, winning streaks, and fortuitous coincidences that together torture common sense. But as in that Peggy Lee song, I still keep asking, "Is that all there is?" Are we, individually, mere statistics—a car accident stat here, a heart attack stat there, a crime stat or a lottery winner stat—simply because X-number of anything is predicted to happen? Is the energetic force animating all luck merely the dry, lifeless law of probabilities?

Peering Beneath Incredible Streaks of Luck

One Sunday in April 1995, an 80-year-old homeless man leaning on a metal walking stick limped into the Treasure Island Casino in Las Vegas and cashed his $400 social security check. He sat down at one of the casino's five-dollar-minimum-bet blackjack tables and proceeded to play. He began winning immediately, nine out of every ten hands he was dealt, and started increasing the size of his bets. A blackjack dealer, identified as Sal in a later conversation with gambling writer and blackjack expert Frank Scoblete, said the man used no identifiable style of play. "He didn't know how to play. He stood on two deuces and would double down on a six or seven. He'd split fours against a ten. He'd split tens. I mean, the guy was just lucky. He played hands of $2,000 to $5,000 each. I think he took me for $60,000 or $70,000 in a few hours."

Shoeless Joe, as the casino employees nicknamed him, played recklessly and against all the recognized, smart-player rules of blackjack, yet he continued winning over a period of days. He would play three hands at a time with $5,000 maximum bets and still consistently come out ahead. By the end of the weekend he had accumulated $1.6 million in winnings. Casino owner Steve Wynn gave Shoeless Joe a suite of rooms, free meals, cigars and liquor, placed a limousine at his disposal, and assigned bodyguards to his protection. This strategy of keeping Shoeless Joe at the casino so he would continue playing, to eventually invoke the law of averages and the house advantage, worked for Wynn, because Shoeless Joe didn't have the good sense to know when to stop gambling. He had apparently become addicted to all of the attention and adrenaline flow.

Within a week, Shoeless Joe lost nearly all of the money he had won, leaving him with $50,000 or so, and ended up back on the street in this town of shattered dreams. As Scoblete wrote, marveling at what "the lucky bum" achieved in his astonishing run of luck, "This guy wasn't (card) counting, had no strategy, just went with the flow. In his case, doing everything wrong turned out right, in the beginning—until everything wrong turned out wrong in the inevitable end."

Sheila King's story represents another kind of streaking luck. Late one August evening in 1991, the 53-year-old widow was at Caesar's Palace in Las Vegas, playing slot machines with her sister and a cousin. Normally she only played $1 and $5 machines, but this particular evening she had a hunch and decided to enter the casino's VIP high-roller area and play a $500 per pull machine. She wasn't a wealthy person. A native of Miami Beach, she had moved to Los Angeles to be near her two grown daughters after her husband, a jeweler, died of cancer. She simply enjoyed the thrill of playing slots, and risking $500 on a single pull of the machine; an act that would give most of us more cautious folk a severe bout of anxiety, somehow made impulsive sense to her in the moment.

So maybe you can imagine what happened next. King hit a $250,000 jackpot. While waiting for casino executives to write out her check, she casually reached over and played an adjoining slot machine. She won $50,000 more. Still waiting for her check, she played a third machine and hit another $50,000 jackpot, all within just a few minutes. "My knees hit the floor," King later told a *New York Times* reporter. "I don't know how I was breathing." Don Guglielmino, then senior vice president of Caesar's, was equally stunned. "I have never seen anybody play as lucky as she did."

For Sheila King this was but an opening act in her reign as undisputed queen of the Vegas slots. From this night forward she only played the $100 and $500 machines, and over the next three years her success was nothing short of phenomenal. On New Year's Eve of 1993, she raked in $1.3 million in slot winnings. Each time she played, often for hours at a time, a casino employee stood nearby holding income tax forms for her to fill out. Casino executives lavished attention and gifts on her, such as the new $85,000 Mercedes-Benz that Caesar's executives presented her with as an inducement—as if she really needed one—to continue playing.

To protect her lucky streak, Ms. King demanded that Caesar's, MGM Grand, and The Hilton, her favorite play spots, all follow a series of guidelines when she was in their casinos. If she stopped playing her favorite machines to take a meal or sleep break, casino personnel were to keep other players away until she returned. Most importantly for her, no technicians could work on her machines unless she was present and observing their actions, a precaution

she took because of concerns that the slot payouts could be manip-
ulated to turn the hot machines she had intuited into cold, black
holes.

Her reign as slot queen came to a flashpoint end in 1994, not as
the result of losses, but due to what she perceived to be a pattern
of breached trust. Apparently, her favorite casinos were no longer
making certain machines exclusively available to her, and technicians had done maintenance on them in her absence. She filed
lawsuits against Caesar's and the Las Vegas Hilton making this
accusation, and filed a complaint with the Nevada Gaming Control
Board accusing the MGM Grand of rigging slot machines to douse
the fire of her win streak. She experienced nothing but bad luck
and frustration, however, in the courts and before the gaming commission, which sided with the casinos.

Though he wasn't necessarily referring to Sheila King, the observations offered by gaming writer Michael Konik would seem to
have possible application to anyone blessed with consistent luck
over a long period of time. "Casinos are considered private businesses and by law may choose whom they will and won't serve,"
wrote Konik in his book, *The Man With the $100,000 Breasts . . . and
other gambling stories*. "Whether you're a $5 or a $100 bettor, if you
play the game too well, you'll be asked to leave."

Archie Karas, a Greek immigrant, arrived in Las Vegas with $50
to his name in 1993. He managed to borrow $10,000 and doubled
that money in a few hours playing poker at the Mirage Casino. He
then went on a streak of luck, a "run," winning $2 million over two
weeks playing poker at Binion's Horseshoe Casino in downtown
Las Vegas. He parlayed some of that money to play dice at Binion's,
collecting $1.6 million, then $1.3 million, then another $4 million
in separate playing sessions. He returned to the poker table and
won $7 million more. Within a few months he had amassed $17
million in winnings.

In 1985, Robert Bergstrom, a real estate developer from Austin,
Texas, placed a $777,000 bet on the pass line of a craps table at
Binion's Horseshoe Casino. An elderly lady rolled the dice and dou-

bled Bergstrom's money. A few weeks later Bergstrom returned and bet $548,000 on the pass line, and once again an elderly lady, apparently a different one, rolled the dice and doubled his money.

An Hawaiian named Stanley Fujitake rolled fifty winners in a row playing craps over a three-hour period at the California Casino in Las Vegas. In 1950 a man playing dice at The Desert Inn in Las Vegas won 28 consecutive throws, beating odds of 10 million to one. At Monte Carlo a roulette wheel came up on "even" 28 times in a row, prompting someone to calculate that odds should dictate this would happen only once in every 500 years of play in that casino. Australian media mogul Kerry Packer won $26 million playing blackjack at the MGM Grand, which works out to $200,000 a hand playing six hands at a time. Not long afterwards, in August 2000, Packer lost $20 million in a three-day losing streak at the Bellagio Casino.

Here is how gaming book author Michael Konik describes the lucky streaks experienced by Karas, Bergstrom, Fujitake, and so many others: "The way most dice players make a fortune is by catching what math mavens call a 'favorable deviation from the norm.' This means that in an infinite string of random numbers, a certain preordained quantity of sevens, elevens, and other numbers will be rolled, approximately as many losers as winners. If you're fortunate enough to make your bets during a period of heavy clustering of winning numbers—otherwise known as a 'hot streak'—the results can be sublimely gratifying."

Dozens of people are repeat state lottery jackpot winners. Here are just a few examples. Joseph Patrick Crowley won $2.4 million in the Ohio lottery in 1987 and retired to Florida. On Christmas Day of 1993, the 66-year-old Crowley won the Florida lottery, this time for $20 million. (Less than two weeks earlier, the woman who would sell Crowley his winning Florida ticket, stationery shop owner Evelyn Weingarten, reportedly had a premonition that Crowley would win and told him so.) Another two-time lottery jackpot winner is convenience store owner Evelyn Marie Adams, who beat odds of *one in 17 trillion* by winning the New Jersey lottery twice in a four-month period during late 1985 and early 1986, taking home

$3.9 million and $1.5 million. Don Whitman Jr. won $2 million in the 1989 Colorado lottery and another $2.2 million in the same state just two years later.

You may wonder, as I did, what do odds against chance of one in 17 trillion really mean? Since I will be using odds-against-chance references throughout this book, I asked former Bell Labs scientist Dean Radin to provide a definition that we math laymen can better understand. Let's say you are playing a slot machine and the odds against chance of winning a jackpot are 10,000 to 1. "Odds of 10,000 to 1 means that if you did the same thing repeatedly (this includes anything that has an uncertain outcome), you'd have to do it 10,000 times to see the results you actually observed. On a slot machine, if you only did one play and hit a jackpot with 10,000 to 1 odds, that's very impressive. If you were able to perform similar stunts repeatedly, then there is no doubt that something very unusual is going on."

As that Rod Stewart song goes, some guys do have all the luck! Stock car driver Kenny Smith of El Monte, California, became a candidate as poster boy for that tune on the night of September 16, 1994, as he competed in the regional stock car races at the Saugus Speedway. First, Smith won the trophy dash, then he captured his heat race, and then he won the main event. This victory gave him the season points championship. At almost the exact instant that the 46-year-old Smith took the checkered flag, the California lottery drawing was held. Smith and his wife, Marylou, had their Quickpick numbers selected for a $22.8 million payday.

For speed of another sort in winning a multiple lottery jackpot, it will be hard ever to top Angelo and Maria Gallina of the San Francisco Bay area, who won the California lottery *twice in an hour*! On November 20, 2002, Angelo, a 78-year-old retired railroad machinist, and 65-year-old Maria won $126,000 in the seven P.M. Fantasy Five lottery game. An hour later, with the eight P.M. drawing for SuperLotto Plus, they struck it rich with a $17 million jackpot. They selected their numbers for both games using a plastic gadget, purchased for $10 at a drugstore, with tiny numbered balls inside that fall into slots to provide lottery numbers. The odds of

₅ two state lottery drawings on the same day were later cal-
.ated at *1 in 24 trillion.* That's right. A 24 followed by 12 zeros.

A three-time lottery winner is Donald Smith of Wisconsin, who
won that state's SuperCash game in May 1993, in June 1994, and
again in July 1995, collecting $250,000 each time. His odds against
chance for winning three times in two years has been calculated in
the quadrillions to one. Warrick Woodard, a career navy seaman,
was a three-time winner of California's Big Spin lottery drawing,
winning $10,000 in April 1988, then $1 million just a month later,
and finally $40,000 in January 1989. On the California Lottery Web
site, where a page of stories describes lottery winners, the following
statement appears: "All of these stories of people experiencing
chance happenings of fortunate events are truly amazing and yet
our winners usually tell us they knew someday their Lottery numbers would be picked." Were all of these winners being delusional
to harbor feelings or expectations of success? Do some streaks of
luck defy even the most elastic applications of probability theory?

If It Wasn't for Bad Luck

"I am Fortune's fool."—William Shakespeare, *Romeo and Juliet*

It is often said that your chances of winning a state lottery are
about the same as your odds of being struck by lightning. So how
do we explain this defiance of odds? During his thirty-six years as a
forest ranger in Virginia's Shenandoah National Park, Roy Sullivan
survived being hit by lightning *seven times,* making him a distinguished veteran of being simultaneously lucky and unlucky. He lost
a big toenail to a strike in 1942; a hit in 1969 singed off his eyebrows; his hair was set afire in 1972 and 1973. The lightning often
singled him out from groups of people, as if he were a human lightning rod. Once a lightning bolt came arcing down from a small
cloud, on an otherwise cloudless day, and the hit knocked him ten
feet into the air. Despite his bad luck at attracting nature's electric-

ity and his good luck in surviving, Sullivan apparently never won a state lottery. He was one of thousands of federal and state forest rangers who spend most of their time outdoors, a career that automatically increases the chances of being electrocuted. So what could have set Sullivan apart from his colleagues? Why did probability theory, so attentive to large numbers and generally so blind to individuals, fail to embrace this particular forest ranger?

Let's examine the common public assumption that a link exists between your odds of winning the lottery and being zapped by lightning. If you remain indoors during every storm, obviously your odds of being struck are much less than if you scurry out into open spaces and pretend to be a tree every time you hear a clap of thunder. But unlike the randomness of lottery drawings, in which every ticket has an equal chance of winning, your chance of getting struck by lightning, points out statistician Mike Orkin, "indicates only what fraction of the population has been struck over a given period, not how likely it is to happen to you."

Some events are so rare that probability theory would have to be written by the creator of *The Twilight Zone* television series for it to be truly relevant. Imagine trying to calculate your odds of surviving a free fall without a parachute from a height of 33,000 feet—more than five miles up. A 22-year-old Yugoslav Airlines flight attendant, Vesna Vulovic, achieved that feat in 1972, when a bomb blew apart the airliner she was unlucky enough to be flying in while at 33,000 feet. She was in the tail section of the plane when it exploded. She rode the tail section down for five miles and then it hit, at an angle, a snowy mountain slope in a forest of Czechoslovakia and slid like a sleigh. Everyone else on the plane perished. Her good luck at surviving bad luck may qualify as a miracle.

The next highest plunge record for falling without a chute belongs to Lieutenant I. M. Chissov, a Soviet pilot who dropped from 22,000 feet after his plane was damaged during a dogfight with German pilots in 1942. He struck the ground a glancing blow on the edge of a snow-covered ravine, much like the flight attendant, and then slid. He suffered damage to his spine and pelvis, but otherwise survived to tell the tale. As if to underscore the durability and luck of the Slavs, a report surfaced in 2002 of a Yugoslav Army paratrooper who survived a drop from 3,300 feet after both his main and spare parachutes failed to open. Forty-year-old Dragan Curcic plunged through the roof of an army building and escaped with minor cuts and bruises.

So, based on what we know about the sometimes contorted reasoning inherent in the laws of probability, the conclusion we might draw from the foregoing goes like this—of all the ethnic groups plummeting to earth in free fall from great heights, chance odds make it inevitable that one group would have more "luck" surviving than the others. For whatever reason, it just happens to be people of Slavic origin. Short of a formal experiment, selecting a certain number of adventurous folk representing all the world's major ethnic groups and simultaneously pushing them out of a plane so we can compare their conditions after splattering, we will have to content ourselves with the mathematical assurance that probability judges best.

For a poignant take on the old bad luck adage "when it rains it pours," we have only to think about the unfortunate Roy Dennis, a 60-year-old Englishman from Hampshire who was visiting his son, Edward, during a 2002 vacation in New Zealand. Determined to show his dad a good time, Edward booked a skydiving plane outside Auckland. On hitting the ground after jumping, Roy snapped his ankle and his son had to rush him to a hospital for emergency surgery. Roy left the hospital in a wheelchair. The following day Edward took Roy to a local aquarium. As he pushed his dad past one of the tanks, a puffer fish jumped out and flopped onto his dad, severely biting him. Roy ended up back at the same hospital for a tetanus shot. Still intent on showing his dad a good time before their reunion ended, Edward took Roy to an adventure park the next day. Park staffers placed the wheelchair-bound Roy in a special car for the tour. The chair wasn't secured properly and broke free during the ride, sending Roy crashing into a window and breaking his nose. He was rushed back to the hospital for his third visit in forty-eight hours. "I feel like a jinx," Edward confessed in a newspaper interview after his father was safely back in England.

"Accidents are one of the most common and familiar forms of bad luck," writes Nicholas Rescher in *Luck: The Brilliant Randomness of Everyday Life*. "The system demands, as it were, a certain number of sacrifices, and they come out on the wrong side of (life's) lottery."

Anything that can happen, and can be predicted under the laws of probability, eventually *will* happen. (And, as we have seen, some events not normally predicted by the theory also occur.) Illustrating this point, a professor of statistics at England's University of Warwick, Dr. Tom Leonard, told this story in 1974 about a new colleague who, in his first lecture at the university, was describing the laws of probability to his students. While making a point about chance odds he pulled a coin from his pocket and tossed it into the air. In Leonard's words, "It landed on a polished floor, spun around a few times, and to a thunderous applause came to rest—vertically on its edge!" A statistician later calculated the odds against chance at one billion to one for a coin to land on its edge after being thrown. As we will see in a later chapter, this incident qualifies as one of those meaningful coincidences called "synchronicity" that stretch the elastic properties of probability theory to its breaking point.

The Hidden Variable of Consciousness

A Las Vegas gambler named Major A. Riddle wrote *The Weekend Gambler's Handbook*, a book that became somewhat of a legend in gambling circles of the 1970s. In it he recommended that gamblers test their luck by placing a few small bets to see how their luck was running that day, and only place larger bets if their luck seemed good. Probability theorists countered that Riddle was promoting superstition because the odds of winning your next bet have nothing to do with your previous success. As a result of coincidence alone, contends statistics professor Edmund Kern, some people will feel that their superstitious practices or actions are justified because the laws of probability sometimes make it seem as if superstitions have had the intended lucky effect. But Riddle was undeterred by these sorts of critiques. After decades of experience as a gambler himself, and being an astute observer of other gamblers, he insisted that runs of luck can be seen, or felt, in advance, and "within certain limits can be managed."

Probability theorists all seem to agree that long streaks of luck in people's lives, even *lifelong* runs of luck, can be predicted to occur with a frequency that should sober—if not immunize—us against feeling any awe or surprise. Lifelong luck! Ponder that for a moment. As one of about six billion human beings on planet Earth, the laws of probability have selected you and X-number of other sentient beings to defy the odds and to experience, for your entire charmed life, nothing but lucky breaks and good fortune. Most of us could forgive that lucky person for counting their blessings by embracing the superstitious belief that their extraordinary fortune had been bestowed, not by a mathematical theory, but by a Higher Power, a God, or by the accumulation of good karmas from previous lives.

But can this theory really explain all extraordinary streaks of luck? Is it possible that intuition provides the key to another way of understanding how luck operates in our lives? Can the probability terms "clustering" and "standard deviation from chance" really explain all of the "coincidences" of lucky streaks? Is it possible that coincidence operates, at times, independently from probability theory? Is there another set of more elastic laws to consider?

The late British philosopher Arthur Koestler spent much of his life formulating these sorts of questions, and in his book, *The Roots of Coincidence*, he came to this conclusion: "Probability theory is the offspring of paradox wedded to mathematics. But it works. The whole edifice of modern physics relies on it, business relies on it. And it works with uncanny accuracy where large numbers of events are considered en masse. That is precisely the reason why, when a large series of events persistently deviates from chance expectation, we are driven to the conclusion that some factor other than chance is involved." (Koestler is referring here to many years of parapsychological research, which we will examine in Part Two, in which results show evidence for precognition and other apparent extrasensory abilities, but which have been dismissed by probability theorists as statistical flukes of coincidence.)

A scientist named Hans Primas, with the Laboratory of Physical Chemistry in Zurich, Switzerland, identified some of the problems with probability theory in a 1999 issue of the *Journal of Scientific Exploration*. "Conceptually more important than statistical descriptions are individual descriptions which refer to individual chaotic processes," wrote Primas. Probability has "a purely mathematical meaning," and that creates "important problems which require a discussion of single random events or of individual chaotic functions. . . . There are no reasons to expect that every chance event is governed by statistical laws of any kind. . . . We have to ask under what conditions the usual 'laws of chance' are valid." In particular, this scientist objected to the idea that probability theory is objective, and thus automatically valid, because it always is "independent or dissected from any human considerations."

There appears to be no doubt, at least in my mind, that the laws of probability are securely fastened to, and helping to guide, nature's web and our consensus reality. Chance does seem to be governed by general principles. Yet, exceptions do seem to arise, and subtle flaws may exist in the allegedly immutable laws of probability. While the mathematical theory works elegantly on paper, and works widely in practice, it doesn't take into account the "hidden variable" of human consciousness.

Our brain's thoughts and patterns of thought don't respect cause and effect or other tenets of probability theory. "Some thoughts flow by association, one from the other," observes the British physicist F. David Peat, "while others emerge out of a common ground or even appear to be quite unconnected. Our inner world does not fulfill the three criteria on which causality is based: events are not clearly distinguished nor are they independent; there is no clear flowing of influence from one event to the next; time is not linear and unambiguous." Professor Peat goes on to note how patterns formed in the unconscious mind are "accompanied by physical patterns in the outer world."

Probability theory laws help us describe how collections of random events can add up to large-scale certainties, but the theory cannot tell us *why*. "The mystery of probability theory is why it works," wrote Arthur Koestler, "but nobody in his right mind would deny that it works."

Yet, the theory has built-in limitations. It has no answers, for example, to some of the gambling questions we might raise, such as: When do I start betting? When should I stop betting? How long will my streak of luck last?

You may have once heard in a classroom, as I did, this mind game promoted as a so-called general truth-of-probability theory. It was first advanced by a member of the British Association for the Advancement of Science and goes like this: if you placed six monkeys in a room and had them pecking away on six typewriters, they would eventually produce, by chance alone, the text of Shakespeare's *Hamlet*. Some enterprising mathematicians tried to calculate the actual odds of this happening, and concluded that it would take even six exceptionally smart monkeys—each typing ten strokes per second—*billions of years* just to produce one phrase, "To be or not to be," by chance. Even then, by producing just those few words, that little group of six monkeys would have been the luckiest non-human critters on the planet.

Intention sometimes throws a monkey wrench into probability theory. For instance, I had the recurring image of those three white sevens in my mind before driving to the Konocti casino with the willful intent of winning on a specific slot machine (as described in the Introduction), and subsequently won with three white sevens on that machine. How can probability theory possibly explain that? How can the theory embrace me knowing that seven would be the Mega number picked a few hours later in the lottery? Oh, I'm sure the theorists will talk in terms of the odds of my successfully acting on this image as opposed to other images that might have come up in my mind. But wait a minute! That image of the three white sevens was *the only time in my life I had ever experienced such a vision!* If it was a lucky coincidence, then it had the apparent significance of those six monkeys writing Shakespeare! There is a point at which this whole exercise of probability speculation becomes a theater of the absurd.

So probability theory, no matter how hard its hardest-core proponents may try, cannot predict everything related to chance. There may be plans for us, individually and collectively, which transcend our rational capacity to comprehend. "Either there are physical processes which cause psychic happenings," the Swiss psychologist Carl Jung once said, "or there is a preexistent psyche which organizes matter." As we will see more clearly in Part III of this book, these threads of an idea lead us into the fabric of a spiritual philosophy about fate known as predestination and karma.

Since every lucky event in our lives that isn't orchestrated by our own will is dismissed as mere coincidence by probabilists, we would be well served to look at whether this marriage of luck and coincidence is really one of convenience. As Carl Jung framed our inquiry, cause and effect "is a statistical truth," one produced by probability theory, yet "it holds good only on average and thus leaves room for exceptions." It is in that realm, the realm of exceptions, that we find a doorway into life's vibrant garden of seemingly magical possibilities.

CHAPTER 3

Reading Patterns of Coincidence

"There is no such thing as chance, and what we regard as blind circumstance actually stems from the deepest source of all."
—Johann Friedrich Von Schiller (1759–1805)

Imagine a realm or zone where fiction and reality merge, where life imitates art, where actors following a script are acted upon by life, and you have a glimpse into the odd circumstances surrounding a now-defunct television series about chance and fate called *Strange Luck*, a production that serves as a sort of metaphorical reference point for this book. The storyline of this FOX network series—which aired in 1995 and 1996—seemed straightforward. A newspaper photojournalist named Chance [played by the actor D. B. Sweeney] who as a child had been the lucky lone survivor of a plane crash, finds himself constantly challenged (blessed?) by fate as a result of his own special powers of intuition.

Chance became the right person in the wrong place in each of the seventeen episodes that FOX aired. His gift of lucky timing placed him in situations where he had to take action to save people, and oftentimes himself, from the curious connivances of their own folly, or from the sometimes cruel contrivances of fate complicated by all manner of coincidences. The creator of this series and its executive producer, Karl Schaefer, by his own admission, took themes and pages from his own experience to inspire the scripts and the characters this series brought to life.

It is the real unorchestrated synchronicities (meaningful coincidences) at work behind the camera before and during the production of this series that I find most intriguing. Karl Schaefer grew up in Bellflower, California, a suburb of Los Angeles, in the same neighborhood as Chris Carter, creator of the hugely popular *X-Files* television series, and though they were only a year apart in age, neither knew the other at the time. When *Strange Luck* began filming in Vancouver, British Columbia, its production facilities were located on the same lot as those of the *X-Files* cast and crew, which gave Schaefer and Carter an opportunity to get to know each other for the first time. The significance of these synchronicities, of their common personal backgrounds, of the placement together of their two shows, of each show having a similar *Twilight Zone*-type of theme, wasn't lost on either man.

During a summer press tour promoting *Strange Luck* in 1995, Schaefer gave reporters an insight into his own sources of inspiration. "The premise of the show in a strange way is a little bit autobiographical. I mean, things happen to me all the time, weird stuff. And I have no reason that I can put on it, other than I think I am looking for it. If you go through life, there's a million little coincidences that we all swing through every day, and if you take every one and spin it toward yourself and say, is this something I need to get involved in? Is this something I'm responsible for? Then you're going to get involved in a lot more strange occurrences and incidents."

A reporter asked Schaefer to elaborate on some of his own strange luck experiences. "Well, let's see, I am on the way, driving from the airport into the office, and upon arriving in Vancouver the first day I got in an accident. In the past, I've pulled a woman off a bridge who was trying to jump onto the Santa Ana Freeway, saw a woman drowning in the Los Angeles riverbed and some friends and I weren't able to save her but we saved a companion of hers. Just, you know, things happen to me. I've probably dialed 911 more times than just about anybody in L.A. Sometimes I would call 911 two or three times in a night, just going, 'Yeah, there's another

here screaming.' I think that's what drove me to write
...a. It's like wondering, why does anything happen to anybody? What is that about?"

Real life imitated art numerous times during production of the
series. While driving home from the set in Vancouver one night,
D. B. Sweeney witnessed a car slide out of control and into a la-
goon. Much as he did in similar scenes featured in the show,
Sweeney called 911 and then handed his phone to a woman bystander so she could describe their location to the police. Sweeney
went into action to rescue the victim and assisted the driver out of
the wreckage and to the shore as the vehicle submerged. Sweeney
returned to retrieve his phone and discovered that the bystander
didn't speak English, so she had been unable to communicate with
the 911 operator. By "coincidence," a police cruiser happened to
pass by at that moment and offered assistance.

Before this incident, during the series promotion tour, Sweeney
had this to say about the art of attracting good luck into his own
life: "You have to set the table for it. To have a great party, it's important how you light the room, where you put the chairs. The
same is true if you want good luck. The room of your life needs to
be in order if you want magic to enter it."

The paradox of coincidence, much like the paradox of luck, is
that once we begin looking for it, once our conscious or unconscious mind starts reflexively scanning the "event horizon," we see
it replicate in patterns uniquely meaningful to us. If we extrapolate
from this observation, we see that the same paradox applies to our
entire species and to all life on Earth.

Luck: A Paradox

To both astronomers and biologists, the Universe, planet Earth,
and the human species exist only because of a long, complex, and
extraordinary series of very lucky coincidences. Their scientific debate isn't about the number or even the nature of the coincidences
that helped evolve the known universe and guide the evolution of

our species. What they can't agree on is whether the coincidences, taken together, have an underlying purpose and transcendent meaning. Do they constitute meaningful evidence for a grand design and a cosmic designer, or do these coincidences amount to nothing more than a byproduct of random chance events?

Physicists and cosmologists highly regarded in their field, like Paul Davies and John Archibald Wheeler, have expressed astonishment at the "coincidences," or intentional design, that produced on Earth circumstances so congenial for life, circumstances such as just the right mix of chemicals, the right orbiting distance from the sun, and on and on. These scientists wonder why the entire universe is set up in such a precise, delicate, highly improbable way. The list of cosmic coincidences is long and often technical, so I won't repeat it here, but suffice it to say, in the words of physicist Davies, "These coincidences are necessary for our existence and this fact is surely one of the most fascinating discoveries of modern science."

The debate over cosmic meaning mirrors the set of questions we each must eventually answer for ourselves in connection with the coincidences occurring in our respective lives. Beyond ordinary coincidences, notes psychotherapist Robert H. Hopcke, most of us have "experienced a different kind of coincidence, a confluence of events that shakes up. . . . We can see and feel a significance in the randomness. . . . It is the meaningfulness of such chance events which makes a synchronistic coincidence different from other sorts of coincidences." Some are meaningful because their occurrence seems so extremely improbable, while others have meaning because there is an uncanny parallel between our internal state of mind and the external occurrence of the event.

Should we regard those patterns of serendipitous events that periodically arise to spice up our ordinary existence—first called "synchronicities" by Swiss psychologist Carl Jung—as having a symbolic or even literal meaning, one that deserves our serious attention and contemplation? Or should we simply dismiss coincidences as odd but meaningless aberrations, and judge ourselves harshly as superstitious if we put any stock in them?

ere is a palpable link between synchronicity and destiny," writes Phil Cousineau in his book on meaningful coincidences, *Soul Moments*. "It is no mere coincidence that the word "weird" is often used to describe the experience of synchronicity since it comes from "wyrd," the Anglo-Saxon word for fate."

Carl Jung claimed that synchronicities, the patterns of meaningful coincidences, occur much more frequently than probability theory can, within reason, predict. To Jung that meant an unknown force was seeking to impose a universal order on random events. Early in his career, after breaking with his mentor, Sigmund Freud, Jung found himself becoming intrigued with "the problem of synchronicity," as he put it, when he kept "coming across connections which I simply could not explain as chance groupings or 'runs.' What I found were 'coincidences' which were connected so meaningfully that their 'chance' occurrence would be incredible."

Jung attributed the genesis of his ideas about synchronicity to a series of dinner conversations he had with Albert Einstein in Switzerland during the period 1909 to 1913. "Professor Einstein was my guest on several occasions at dinner," wrote Jung later in his life. "Those were the very early days when Einstein was developing his first theory of relativity, and it was he who first started me off thinking about a possible relativity of time as well as space, and their psychic conditionality."

In 1985, years after Jung died, science writer Rudy Rucker, in the magazine *Science*, concurred with Jung's view that some synchronicities seem beyond chance. "Statistically, of course, one expects a certain number of coincidences to occur. Still, one sometimes gets the feeling that life exhibits meaningful coincidences more often than the mere law of averages would predict. Synchronicity suggests a hidden force that manipulates our space and time."

British physicist F. David Peat calls synchronicity the "jokers in nature's pack of cards" because they refuse to play by the rules, and a "bridge between mind and matter" that exposes "a tiny flaw in the fabric of all that we have taken for reality." Peat rightly characterizes the problem we face in our daily lives as one of differentiating between events occurring out of pure chance and those that represent "a mysterious underlying affinity," one that deviates from normal probability. Carl Jung made this distinction by theorizing that "what truly separates a synchronicity from a mere coincidence is its inherent meaning."

Synchronicity has been one of my own areas of interest. In my experience, the more I have paid attention to synchronicities, and the more meaning I found in them, or attached to them, the more they seemed to occur. I began collecting examples from human history that seem to illustrate the idea of harmonies emerging from the seemingly chaotic interactions of human consciousness and the material world. These harmonic coincidences give the appearance of, or mimic the attributes of, what we call luck or miracles.

Meaning and Historical Events

At a macro level, we find coincidences affecting our interpretation, if not the actual course, of human history in a variety of meaningful ways. New Testament accounts of the crucifixion of Jesus Christ describe how the sun turned to darkness while Jesus was dying on the cross, and the moon turned to blood just after his death. Religious scholars later calculated that these events probably occurred on a Friday in April of the year 33 A.D.

A little more than 1,950 years following the crucifixion, two Oxford University scientists, writing in the British journal *Nature*, presented compelling evidence for an extraordinary coincidence occurring on the most probable execution date. Through a series of calculations into astronomical history, plotting the incidence of lunar eclipses, these scientists found that on the first Friday of April, 33 A.D., a partial eclipse of the moon was visible to the residents of Jerusalem. This eclipse would have been seen as "blood red" because a massive dust storm earlier in the day, documented in Roman records, spewed so many dust particles into the sky that the rising lunar eclipse turned bright red. This same dust storm had blotted out the sun during the afternoon, accounting for the eerie daylight darkness that observers reported as Jesus died.

What are we to make of this? For Christian believers in the divinity of Christ, these scientific findings may simply reaffirm what they already believed through the message of their faith—that God created the dust storm to produce the reported effects to inspire a sense of wonder and mark the passage of his only begotten son. For unbelievers and probability theorists, these events are "mere" or "sheer" coincidence, holding significance only to the extent that one chooses to attach meaning. "The Jesus myth got lucky," an atheist might say.

In southern Mexico during the sixteenth century, the Aztec people preserved a legend from centuries earlier describing the career of a priest-ruler, Topiltzin Quetzalcoatl (a name translated as Our Prince, Feathered Serpent), who had disappeared to the east with a group of followers. Aztec tradition held that in the year 1 Reed, a year on the Aztec calendar corresponding to 1519 A.D., this exalted ruler would return from the east and reclaim his throne. In the year 1519, of course, Hernan Cortes and his small band of Spanish colonist-soldiers landed on the eastern shores of the Aztec empire, were immediately mistaken as the fulfillment of the prophecy, and as a result were able to conquer the Aztecs despite being outnumbered thousands to one. As nations and peoples, Spain and the invaders got very lucky, while the Aztecs descended into prolonged misfortune. (It strikes me that maybe if we accept the possibility of precognition, this legend, because it involved such a specific date, could have been a prophecy about enslavement rather than liberation. Subsequent generations of Aztecs simply distorted or misinterpreted some Aztec sage's glimpse into the future.)

From folktales and fables we find multiple appearances of the same basic stories in widely separated cultures. These societies apparently never had contact during the period when their similar stories independently emerged. By way of example, scattered across four continents there are over 300 worldwide variations on the theme of Cinderella, the classic story of good luck and personal transformation. Or consider the Biblical story of Joseph, and his brothers who sold him into slavery. A tale closely resembling this one was firmly entrenched in Polynesian folktelling tradition centuries before any islander had contact with a Bible or Bible stories.

Author Idries Shah, in his 1979 book, *World Tales: The Extraordinary Coincidence of Stories Told in All Times, in All Places*, offered a fascinating premise about why these coincidences accumulated. "Folktales have a secondary, inner significance, which is rarely glimpsed consciously, but which nevertheless acts powerfully on our minds." He speculates that such stories have "been used intentionally from time immemorial by certain groups interested in spiritual development."

Because human brains across all cultures and ethnic groups are hardwired the same way, possessing much of the same genetic programming, authors such as Carl Jung, in his theory of the collective unconscious, and Joseph Campbell, in his comparative studies of the symbols and themes common to our mythologies, have argued that these sorts of "coincidences" should be expected. Consciousness itself seems naturally inclined to produce an intricate web of order and meaning from the midst of the chaos and the uncertainty of life and nature.

Personal Dimensions of Synchronicity

Coincidences occurring at the micro level of a single or a few human lives are no less puzzling, and are often more complex, than the examples we have just considered from the macro level. Sometimes "coincidence" and bad luck merge in a manner seeming to underscore the old adage that "what you fear most in life will eventually get you."

An oracle warned Aeschylus, the playwright of ancient Greece, that he should be wary of storms because "a blow from Heaven" would one day end his life. He heeded that warning, according to reports handed down to us, by always cowering indoors during storms. But he died from a blow out of Heaven anyway, on a sunny day in 456 B.C., when a passing eagle dropped a giant tortoise on his head. A cynic might call this "an unlucky break." Yet, I wonder if we don't sometimes help attract our good luck and bad luck according to the intensity of our emotional attachment to our beliefs. Can we sometimes, individually or collectively, set up a vibratory field that obeys the laws of attraction?

If we consider the lives of the fewer than fifty men who have held the office of President of the United States, we begin to stretch the boundaries of probability theory when we contrast just two of them, Abraham Lincoln and John F. Kennedy. You have probably read or heard the details before. Both Lincoln and Kennedy were assassinated on a Friday in the presence of their wives. Both were succeeded by southern Democrat senators named Johnson. Both presidents lost a son while living in the White House. Lincoln's secretary, named Kennedy, warned him not to attend the theater the night he was shot. Kennedy's secretary, named Lincoln, had a similar premonition and warned him not to travel to Dallas. Lincoln was killed in Ford's Theater, while Kennedy died in a Lincoln car made by the Ford Motor Company. Booth shot Lincoln in a theater and fled to a warehouse. Oswald shot Kennedy from a warehouse and fled to a theater. Both Lincoln and Kennedy have seven letters in their name. Both were dedicated to the civil rights cause of African-Americans. And the list goes on and on in a seemingly endless series of connections between the two men.

Ordinary people also experience synchronistic rendezvous with destiny that temporarily catapult them onto the world stage. Leonard Dawe was a schoolteacher in Britain during World War II who wrote the crossword puzzles appearing in the *London Daily Telegraph*. In the months prior to June 6, 1944 (D-Day), the most closely guarded secrets held by British and American military planners were the codewords "Utah" and "Omaha" (the beaches where Allied troops would land), "Mulberry" (the artificial harbor for use after landing), "Neptune" (the naval plan of operations), and "Overlord" (the codeword for the Normandy invasion). Throughout the

month of May 1944, Leonard Dawe thought up (intuited?) ea
these words—Utah, Omaha, Mulberry, Neptune, and Overlord—as
answers to his crossword puzzle in the London newspaper. Dawe
was not a part of the war effort, and he certainly wasn't supposed to
be privy to any state secrets. He immediately came under suspicion
by British intelligence agents as a Nazi spy who used the London
newspaper to transmit espionage information to Germany. Dawe
was fiercely interrogated for many days until British authorities realized he was simply an innocent instrument of a "bizarre coincidence." Dawe had just gotten "lucky" in defying chance.

Carl Jung's collaborator, the physicist Wolfgang Pauli, believed
there were ordering principles in the universe beyond what we can
see and measure, with synchronicity being one such principle.
Pauli first became interested in synchronicity after he discovered an
abstract pattern beneath the surface of atomic matter that determines subatomic behaviors in ways unrelated to the cause-and-
effect laws of our ordinary reality.

Synchronicity, to summarize the various descriptions, remains
a mysterious, little understood, but perfectly natural presence, a
force that somehow brings like together with like, and does so in
a manner inconsistent with any reasonable application of probability theory. Synchronicity resembles an informational glue or a
sort of magnetic attraction that synchronizes events, creates orderly patterns, and enables similar or related things to cluster in
space or time. When we experience streaks of luck we are being
blessed by this clustering effect. In Jung's view, these phenomena
are a special class of natural events, a category ranking alongside
space, time, and causality as universal principles, but also set
apart because they are "the sum of countless individual acts of
creation occurring in time."

Jungian psychotherapist Robert H. Hopcke, in *There Are No
Accidents*, takes us to the brink of a testable theory: "Synchronistic
events urge upon us a view of the world as a unified field in which
one's own experiences and actions are fundamentally connected to
the experiences and actions of others."

Can Our Unconscious Orchestrate Synchronicities?

Consider what happened on September 11, 2002, the first anniversary of the terrorist attacks on New York and Washington, D.C. That night the New York state lottery drawing was held. Three numbers were selected when three levers were pressed, popping up three numbered balls randomly into tubes. The numbers turned out to be 9-1-1. This was the first time in more than a year that the 9-1-1 combination had been selected. Prior to the drawing on 9/11, lottery officials had stopped selling that number combination because so many New Yorkers had purchased it. Commenting to the Associated Press on the one in 1,000 chance of those numbers coming up, University of Buffalo probabilities expert Professor Christopher Rump said: "I'm a bit surprised, but I wouldn't characterize it as bizarre. It's randomness. People tend to read into these things." In another ironic twist on the anniversary day, the Standard & Poor's futures market opened at 911.00 on 9/11, a coincidence that, according to news reports, unsettled traders on the Chicago Mercantile Exchange.

Other examples abound of lottery results mirroring significant public anniversaries or tragic event numbers. The day American Airlines flight 587 crashed off the New York coast, the numbers 5-8-7 came up in the neighboring New Jersey lottery drawing. On the day a ceremony was held at Yankee Stadium in New York honoring baseball legend Mickey Mantle, who wore #7 during his long career, the winning lottery numbers were 777 in New York.

Could these "coincidences" have been induced by our collective attentions? (In Part Two, evaluating research on psi, we will see how group consciousness may have an effect on the random event generators that form the "consciousness" of slot machines.) Physicist F. David Peat, in his book, *Synchronicity: The Bridge Between Matter and Mind*, elaborates on this idea. "Synchronicities are often associated with periods of transformation—for example, births, deaths, falling in love, intense creative work, and even a change of profession. It is as if this internal restructuring produces external resonances, or as if a burst of 'mental energy' is propagated outward into the physical world."

We live in a world "filled with harmonies and coincidences," says science writer Rudy Rucker, "that have no explanation in terms of cause and effect." Synchronicity, by its very nature, suggests the presence of a hidden force that manipulates our reality. One example of harmony Rucker cites, which is suggestive of a hidden force similar to synchronicity, is the mind-boggling experiment that makes it appear as though two subatomic particles, once in contact, continue to communicate with each other as if by telepathy. Scottish physicist John Bell conceived a theorem, based on earlier theoretical speculations by Albert Einstein and two scientific collaborators, demonstrating that if the laws of quantum physics are accurate, subatomic particles, once in contact, will continue influencing each other instantaneously, even if they are separated by millions of light years in distance or thousands of years in Earth time.

Taking Bell's Theorem and applying it beyond subatomic physics into our physical realm of perception, we find a possible mechanism for how seemingly unrelated persons or events can be drawn together and interact in a way that doesn't involve our traditional notions of cause and effect. Some physicists have proposed that the medium of interconnectedness could be an information transfer rather than an energy transfer, because energy, as we understand it, cannot exceed the speed of light to create an instantaneous effect. The organizing principle inherent in information, by contrast, may not be constrained by the speed-of-light barrier. We will learn more about this information theory in Part Two (also see the Appendixes), as scientists grapple for an explanation of parapsychological effects.

Noted theoretical physicist David Bohm once suggested that people and subatomic particles may be influencing each other because "an implicate order" exists connecting everything in the universe, even the past, present, and future. In Bohm's view, this idea embraces the existence of precognition, telepathy, and other so-

chic" abilities. Bohm further argued that at the sub-
level of reality, cause and effect become an illusion. Carl
g made the same argument about psychic events in our everyday reality. At the quantum level, said Bohm, energy and matter are
indistinguishable, as are waves and particles. As a result, Bohm suspected we live in a holographic universe; our consciousness transcends space and time, and eludes any attempt to measure it as an
energy. Space and time are constructs created by the human mind,
in the scientific view, because we have a need to define a context to
measure the behavior of physical objects in motion. Humans invented time, I have always been fond of saying, to measure our
own mortality, our own inevitable physical decay.

We have at least two ways to utilize synchronicities as signposts
on the road to luck. Psychiatrist Judith Orloff calls synchronicities
"an expression of our psychic rapport with the world around us. I
look to them for guidance. They reaffirm that I'm on the right
path." She uses them in the passive-observer mode of responding
to their occurrence with her intuitive skills of interpretation.

By contrast, an author of books on synchronistic occurrences,
Alan Vaughan, illustrates the active role we can play in the process
with his observation that "our consciousness orchestrates the
chance events in our lives according to our mostly unconscious desires. Belief seems to be a potent factor in the production of incredible coincidences, particularly the miraculous event that occurs by
chance."

Winning at games of chance is often an exercise in synchronicity. Take the playing of slot machines. In ten seconds, the amount
of time between one player leaving a slot machine and another
player sitting down, the microchip in that machine has already
played out hundreds of different number combinations, a few of
which could have yielded winnings if the "Play" button had been
pushed at that instant. As a result, says Frank Scoblete, the author
of numerous books on slot playing, "The winning of a big jackpot
is a synchronistic event—the cojoining of coins in and random
number selected." (In Part Two, we will sort through experimental

evidence of whether slot machine synchronicities can be something more than random chance.)

Can we distinguish between coincidence and effects possibly caused by our own minds? Ironically, parapsychological researchers determine this distinction by using the mathematical theory of probability. "Statistical tables have been developed to evaluate when a series of events falls within the realm of simple chance and when it does not," report Norma Bowles and Fran Hynds, co-authors of *Psi Search*. "When the observed events (psychic effects) deviate widely and consistently from chance expectation, some factor may be presumed to be causing this deviation."

Nature demonstrates a fundamental tendency to create order out of disorder. Why should human consciousness be any different? If the roots of coincidence can be found in parapsychology, as Jung, Koestler, and other eminent figures have proposed, then the roots of luck are also sunk deep into the extrasensory realm.

Luck Secrets: An Overview

My perspective on how our unconscious desires operate in tandem with coincidences underwent an evolution while I conducted interviews for this book. It became clear to me, based on the experiences and insights of certifiably lucky people, that **if we recognize and appreciate the appearance of serendipity and synchronicity in our lives we seem to enhance our chances of being blessed with good fortune.** To some extent, there seems to be a law of attraction at work here—the more we notice something, the more of it we attract into our lives.

Chance occurrences can become the seeds of luck once they are planted in the unconscious mind. There are principles, attitudes, practices, and behaviors that seem vital to lucky people and how they utilize synchronicity in their lives. Usually our ego, and our ego attachments to things and beliefs, cause us to ignore the possible meanings of synchronicities. If we are rigid in life, if we structure our relationships to people and events too narrowly, we take ourselves out of the flow of serendipity.

It is how we respond to synchronistic events, not the events themselves, that usually brings us luck. If we give up the pretense of always being in control, if we surrender to the spontaneous and unpredictable flow of the serendipity that arises, we open ourselves more fully to the blessings of good fortune.

Notes Alan Vaughan, "Synchronicity happens to people when they need it. When you don't need it—when your life is secure and stable—it happens rarely. If you live by your wits or in an insecure profession, you will probably find it happening all the time."

Lucky people are alert to chance encounters and their possible significance. Max Gunther became intrigued with the link between chance, synchronicity, and luck when "I happened to be on the right street corner at the right time where I met the right guy who offered me the right job, an editorship with *Time* magazine, and changed my life."

Psychotherapist Robert Hopcke suggests that **lucky people are those who find value, meaning, and lessons in synchronicities even when they are not what you want to happen.** Synchronicities quite often materialize when we most have our minds made up about what we will or won't accept from life. Lucky people learn to read these signposts and make appropriate course corrections.

"We don't see things as they are, we see them as we are," wrote the French novelist Anaïs Nin. If we are blind to the prospect of magic happening around us and to us, if we are limited by our beliefs or our fears, then we will fail to decipher or heed those fortuitous patterns that periodically coalesce to express life's beneficial plans for us.

PART TWO

PREMONITIONS OF
GOOD FORTUNE

CHAPTER 4

Deciphering Intuitive Hunches

"The intuitive mind is a sacred gift and the rational mind is a faithful servant." —Albert Einstein

On the very day Don Browne's life turned around for the better he was bemoaning how he had hit a dry patch in his fortunes. Jobless, without money for that month's rent, the 25-year-old musician sat with a friend in a Los Angeles restaurant and voiced strong doubts about the wisdom of his choices in life. He had grown tired of the hardships, the hand-to-mouth existence, and it seemed as if nothing came to him anymore without a protracted and frustrating effort.

In the midst of this conversation, Don suddenly felt a "need" to find the men's restroom. It wasn't a physical sensation that motivated him. As he later told me, "I didn't really need to go. I just felt compelled to. It was like I had been hypnotized. I was following some inner voice other than my mind."

He went outside where the restrooms were located. The moment he opened the door he spotted a wad of paper crumpled on the floor. He reached down and picked it up—it was money, many hundreds of dollars, which turned out to have no identifiable owner. This find enabled Don to pay his rent and other bills. It also helped set in motion a chain reaction of events that culminated in Don finding the woman he would marry.

"Finding the money based on an intuitive feeling was confirmation that I could place faith and trust in an ultimate outcome," Don explained. "Everything worked out from then on in my jobs and my finances. As a result of this experience I felt more attuned to recognizing magic when it happens. I got into a flow which was in harmony with the forces in my own life. It was a surrender to the flow, even though it feels so alien to the ego to give up the illusion of control. I had entered a zone, the flow of luck, which to me feels analogous to where I'm at when I'm in the creative flow of writing and playing music. This experience prepared me for meeting Dora, who is now my wife. The instant I met her I had that intuitive feeling of rightness, and I was able to trust the feeling, and act on it, in a way I wouldn't have before finding the money."

Don's story illustrates how intuition transmits "lucky" information spontaneously and concisely, like a news headline or a radio news flash channeled into our consciousness. Intuition often plays the role of our personal border patrol, guarding and regulating the boundaries of our sensory awareness, and sometimes stretching beyond, to communicate messages that help to empower us in decision-making.

The word "intuition" comes from the Latin *intueri*, meaning "to consider, to look on." The *Oxford English Dictionary* defines intuition this way: "The quick perception of truth without conscious attention or reasoning; knowledge from within; instinctive knowledge or feeling." Consulting the *Encyclopedia Britannica*, I found this diplomatic spin: "Intuition is designed to account for just those kinds of knowledge that other sources do not provide."

Sometimes called the "handmaiden of inductive reasoning," intuition functions as a creative channel through which luck often flows. It gives us information or premonitions, onto which an emotional charge is often attached, usually designed to warn us of a threat or danger, or to keep us lucky by providing a feeling or sense of direction and action that we should take. Intuition produces an inner experience variously described as vibes, hunches, gut feelings, a sense of certainty, mental voices, sensations of attraction, affinity, repulsion, or foreboding. We feel it through symptoms in our bodies, typically as an accelerated heartbeat, warmth or tingling in the hands, "goose bumps" on the skin, a sudden inexplicable anxiety, or the sensation of being physically pulled somewhere as if by a magnet.

"Hearing your intuition," writes neuroscientist Mona Lisa Schulz in her book, *Awakening Intuition*, "really requires little more than simply paying attention, even to seemingly random, insignificant, irrelevant thoughts, ideas, sensations, and emotions. Intuition comes to us from unexpected sources at unexpected times. Choosing to hear it or choosing to ignore it can make the difference between health and disease, happiness and unhappiness, a richer or an emptier life."

Premonitions of Danger

During the second World War, British Prime Minister Winston Churchill had numerous premonitions that saved his own life and the lives of many people around him. His wife, Lady Clementine, shared some of these stories with her biographer, who in 1963 produced *My Darling Clementine: The Story of Lady Churchill*. One of the more remarkable premonitions occurred at the height of the "blitz," the German bombing of London.

"Three government ministers were dining with the prime minister. The blitz began as usual, but the party went on and the cook and maid continued working in the kitchen next to a twenty-five-foot-high plate glass window. Suddenly, acting on a premonition, Churchill got up and went into the kitchen. 'Put dinner on a hot-plate in the dining room,' he instructed the butler, and ordered everyone in the kitchen to the bomb shelter. Then he went back to his guests and his dinner. Three minutes later, a bomb hit the house, totally destroying the kitchen."

My friend Donald Altman, a former Buddhist monk and now a psychotherapist, told me about the time he had to learn a lesson the hard way about the need to trust his intuitive early-warning system. While walking through a hotel parking lot one evening in 1993, "I suddenly got the image, the thought, of what if someone tried to rob me. That thought had never come up in me before. As I was playing this scenario in my mind, and imagining myself running away from any would-be robber, I saw a car's headlights go on about two blocks down the street. The car drove toward me and stopped, and a man on the passenger side got out with a large knife. 'Give me your money!' he shouted. There was nowhere for me to run. An internal voice instructed me to throw down my wallet. I did and the robber drove away with it."

Six months later, Donald flew into the Los Angeles airport and boarded a shuttle bus to pick up his car at a long term parking lot. "There were fifteen other people on the shuttle bus. At one of the terminals, a man in his late twenties who didn't carry any luggage stepped aboard the bus. Immediately, I knew he was going to try and rob me. I had told myself if I ever got that intuition again I would act on it. So, instead of getting off the bus where my car was parked, I got off near a vending and rest area where other people congregated. After a few moments of walking toward my car, I looked back and he was right behind me. At that moment, I changed direction and joined others who were waiting in the vending area. Just as quickly, he turned and walked away. Not long after this happened, it came to me that this second experience was a test to see if I had learned to listen to my intuition. It was a lucky thing I did."

Donald's voice of protection, as he calls that aspect of his intuition, spoke up again years later while he was driving from a Buddhist monastery where he had been on a meditation retreat. "I had an intuitive flash, just a very specific feeling, that an accident was about to happen. So, reflexively I slowed down and switched lanes of traffic. Seconds later a car pulled out of a mini-mall and slammed into the car in the lane next to me, just where I would have been if I hadn't slowed and switched lanes."

Educational psychologist Gail Ferguson, in her book, *Cracking the Intuition Code*, tells the following story to illustrate how reliable her own early-warning system has been. She was backing her car out of her garage in 1972 when the words, "the brakes are going to fail" entered her mind. To test this impression, she pressed hard on the brake and the car stopped immediately. She also tested the emergency brake, and it, too, worked fine. But she had learned over the years to trust her intuitive messages.

"Even though there was absolutely no physical indication that the brakes were a concern, I could rely on the 'impression.' It would be accurate. I also had discovered through the years that I would have to figure out what to do next—make a plan."

She had to pick her son up from nursery school, so her plan became one of selecting the safest route among all of the available ways to the nursery school. Her drive went smoothly until a green light quickly turned yellow. She stepped on the brake and nothing happened. The pedal went straight to the floorboard. She tried the emergency brake. It also failed. Meanwhile, she was about to run a red light in a busy intersection.

"I was very calm," Ferguson relates, "probably because I had the forewarning and put myself on alert." She steered the car onto a ten-inch-high median lane divider on her left, and succeeded in halting the car. She had gotten lucky. The premonition had prepared her for what otherwise could have been a catastrophic accident.

How do we separate an intuitive sense of danger from paranoia produced by our imagination? Ferguson offers this advice. "One difference is that imagination grows wild, wicked, and wonderful stories in the head like a cumulus cloud building its vaporous masses of fluff, while an intuitive effect is unwavering truth. You sense danger."

Premonitions of Winning Money

Lucky people often experience an uncanny sense of knowing that good fortune will follow if they act upon their intuitive messages. Take Sue Henley, a 47-year-old Las Vegas resident who won the largest slot machine jackpot in Nevada history, more than $12 million, in April 1997. She had gone to the New York-New York Casino on a hunch after finishing her night shift as a construction inspector on a road project. "I just had a hunch about that particular machine," Henley explained. "I gamble when I have a feeling. I only gamble every few months when the hunch or feeling comes up." Henley's previous gambling experience, just two months earlier, also occurring after she experienced the feeling of being lucky, had rewarded her with a $50,000 jackpot at the Las Vegas Hilton.

One of the more famous lucky hunches in history occurred in 1906, when Jesse Livermore suddenly felt he should sell all of his Union Pacific railroad stock. Without knowing why, he went into his broker's office and sold all of his stock short, even though there was absolutely no rational reason for doing so, and walked out with $300,000, a princely sum in those days. The next day San Francisco had a devastating earthquake that destroyed much of Union Pacific's facilities and plunged the company's stock down to near worthlessness.

When interviewing people who are consistently lucky, I always asked them to provide descriptions of their "hunches" or "intuitive feelings" in as much detail as possible. I wanted a sketch of the range of intuitive symptoms. Forty-seven-year-old crane operator Jim Mello of Vallejo, California, explained how he feels the premonitions in his body. "My heart beats fast, and the adrenaline pumps as if I had won before I actually do win. I feel like I am in a zone."

The first week in August 2002, Mello felt those symptoms and told his wife, Terry, "I feel lucky tonight." They drove to the Twin Pines Casino outside Middletown, California. While still in the parking lot, Mello felt his heart beating faster and the rush of adrenaline, all reinforcing his sense of knowing that he was about to win big money. He found a dollar machine, a three-times multiplier, and using the $60 he had withdrawn from an ATM, played until he hit a $720 jackpot. This was on a Thursday. Three days later, Mello got the feeling again and returned to play the same dollar machine. He got lucky again with an $1,800 jackpot. But the third time was the real charm. On August 29, Mello went back to Twin Pines and on the third pull of the play lever he hit (3) (3) (3) for $2,500, the highest jackpot possible on that machine.

"Three has been my lucky number since childhood," Mello told me the day after winning his last jackpot. "I was attracted to that machine because it was a three-times multiplier. I've been married three times. I'm the third son in my family. Now I've won big on that machine three times."

"I've never had that gut feeling of being in a zone and not won something," Mello assured me. "I'm a recovering alcoholic, so I know addictions and I can separate obsessive-compulsive feelings from the sensation of being in that zone."

An all-time leading lottery winner was Randy Portner of Rome, New York, who won state lottery prizes of up to $50,000 at least *19 times* during the 1970s. "I'd have this feeling there was a winning ticket and I'd act on that feeling," he explained. For more recent examples, consider what some winners of the Oregon state lottery have said. Twenty-year-old Stacey Brooks won $5 million after buying a lottery ticket because "something told me I should." Michael O'Donnell attributes the $7.8 million he won to "receiving a message . . . something told me it was time to get my tickets." When Jerry McGovern claimed his $29 million in a 2002 lottery drawing in California, he told lottery officials, "I always had a feeling I would win someday."

In Texas, Frances Soileau and her husband, Lee, both retired and living in Port Arthur, took home a $6 million jackpot on July 26, 2002, and in the aftermath Frances assured reporters, "I always thought we would win someday." Glenn Smith of Paris, who shared in a $17 million Texas jackpot on April 24, 2002, later declared, "I had such a strong feeling the day before the drawing about winning." A similar confession came from Happy Roberts, the co-owner of a lawn mowing service in Sequin, who said the $20 million he won in 2001 had been felt and then predicted: "I've always told people I was going to win."

Michael Macy was thirty-one years old, an executive in the book publishing industry, when he and an old college friend, Mark, were driving on vacation from New York to California and decided to stop outside Las Vegas at a roadside cafe. Like just about every public facility in Nevada, this cafe had a row of slot machines near the entrance. After eating and paying their bill, Michael and Mark were on the way out when Mark said, "Hey, let's put a quarter in one."

At first Michael thought about saying it would be a waste of time and money. He had never gambled and believed that gambling was irresponsible. But instead, a feeling came over him, a magical feeling, a premonition, as if the outcome had already been determined. Mark put in the quarter, pulled the lever, and more than 100 quarters poured out of the machine, metal clanging loudly onto metal. Everyone in the restaurant seemed to turn in their seats to watch this unfolding scene.

"It felt like our good energy was being reciprocated," Michael explained. "We both laughed because it seemed like such a play. Mark put another quarter in, and this time I pulled the lever. Immediately another hundred or more quarters spilled out. It felt like some greater force or energy was at work and we were just flowing with it, knowing that something good would happen." They left after this second win, interpreting their success as an affirmation of the joy they both felt at renewing an old friendship.

Dorothy Walker, a successful real estate agent with Country Air Properties in Lake County, California, enjoys playing slot machines "for entertainment and relaxation" at Indian casinos and on trips to Reno, Nevada. Quite often she hears a voice—not an auditory voice, but an intuitive voice in her mind—telling her "you should play today," or, "you should play that machine." On a Reno trip she had been watching a particular dollar slot machine in the Comstock Casino. She had a feeling, more like a certainty, that "the next time this machine is vacant I am going to win big on it." After feeding it $30, she hit three sevens, a red, white, and blue combination for $10,000. She surprised herself, her husband, and numerous witnesses by her calm reaction. "I felt a satisfaction," Dorothy told me, "but it came from confidence. I had simply known I was going to hit big on that machine."

On another occasion, while playing dollar slots at Robinson Rancheria, a Pomo Indian casino in Lake County, Dorothy felt herself resonating with a machine, almost as if she had merged with it. "Someone seemed to be standing behind me telling me, over and over, that I was going to win. But there wasn't anyone behind me. It was just the feeling of a presence." She had played only a few minutes when the machine rewarded her with a $1,600 jackpot.

At Konocti Vista, where I conducted much of my research, casino employees marvel at how Dorothy is one of their consistently lucky players. She routinely comes out ahead. "I never go in with the intention of winning, and I don't invest a lot of attachment to outcomes, but I do follow my intuitive hunches. When I don't follow them, I always regret it. I consider myself to be a spiritual person rather than a religious person, and I do count my blessings. I think I'm lucky because I have a great family, my children are healthy, and I've led a good life."

One afternoon at the Twin Pines Casino, I watched a middle-aged woman winning consistently as she alternated among three different dollar machines. She hit two sevens and a doubler on the payline for a $720 jackpot, then moved over to an adjoining machine and began raking in a hundred dollars or more at a time. During the thirty minutes or so that I observed her, the gush of dollar tokens hitting the metal tray sounded like a hard, marble-sized hailstorm pounding the hood of a car. I struck up a conversation and she introduced herself as Margaret. Earlier in the day she had a feeling about these particular machines and had visualized them before walking into the casino. "I also talk to them as I play," she confided. "I try to coax them along."

"Which one are you going to play next?" I asked her.

She pointed to another dollar machine, a three-times multiplier, situated in the corner at the end of a bank of machines. "I have a good feeling about that one."

With me standing behind her as a witness, she went over and sat down at that machine and began feeding it two-dollar tokens. Within several minutes she hit a $400 payout. I gasped in surprise, more excited about the big win than she was. She ascribed her nonchalance to the trust and confidence she had developed in her own intuition.

"How long has this winning streak been going on?"

"Two months," she replied, with a wide smile. "I hit $10,000 on a ten-times machine last week at Cache Creek (another Indian casino about an hour's drive away). That puts me $50,000 ahead in winnings for the year."

"What a streak," I marveled. "What do you attribute it to?"

Her expression turned somber and reflective. "I'm a cancer survivor. My colon cancer is in remission. I never used to win anything at all. But after I went into remission I started getting intuitive feelings about winning. It's like these were blessings being given me. All I have to do is follow the instructions."

For Margaret and many other lucky winners, good fortune cannot be separated from the spiritual component of blessings they believe they have been ordained to receive. As we will explore more thoroughly in Part Three, the spiritual dimension of good fortune involves the clarity of intuition wedded to the power of belief and faith.

Intuition Can Produce Professional Luck

A great believer in following "gut instinct," as he called it, was the late J. Peter Grace, who served as chairman of the chemical corporate giant, W. R. Grace & Company. I had the opportunity to spend a lot of time around Grace in 1983, while I co-wrote a presidential commission report that Grace oversaw for the Reagan administration. Grace liked to tell stories with a common theme of how most of the major decisions in his life, professionally and personally, had been made by "what my stomach tells me." Grace literally felt the rightness or wrongness of choices based on a sharp feeling in his solar plexus. To him those intuitive sensations were as valid as all the facts and statistics the experts and his rational mind could summon.

Paying attention to these physical effects and to the quiet inner voice "is what successful people always do, whether they are conscious of it or not," says psychologist Marcia Emery. "An intuition is not a whim, a good guess, or even blind luck. Intuition is a real force in every human psyche." To underscore her point, she relates a statement once made by Richard DeVos, founder of the Amway Corporation: "The guys that finally rise to the top are a limited group who run on their intuition."

Don Hewitt, longtime producer of the CBS *60 Minutes* program, told Emery that he and his colleagues on the show have always relied on intuition. "All of us live by the gut feeling. Everything is a hunch around here." He admitted as well that stories aired by the broadcast are selected based on their passage of the "sound test" and the "smell test." "You sort of smell them out. You say 'that sounds like it could be great.' And what smells right and sounds right is usually right."

Another story Emery tells in her book, *PowerHunch!*, concerns a General Motors engineer, one of her students when she was teaching at the University of Michigan. He used intuition to accurately pick the winner of every game in the NCAA basketball tournament. "Al silenced his logical mind and brought forth his intuitive mind. As he mentioned the name of each team, he became highly aware of how his taste buds responded. A sour taste always alerted him to the loser. A good taste signaled the winning team."

Both George Washington Carver and Thomas Edison credited most of their ideas for inventions to information received through their intuition. Albert Einstein used this description of how he used intuition in problem-solving: "There comes a leap in consciousness, call it intuition or what you will—the solution comes to you and you don't know how or why."

Two corporate executives who made no secret of their reliance on intuition for luck were William K. Keeler, a longtime board chairman of Phillips Petroleum, and Alexander M. Poniatoff, founder of Ampex Corporation. "Oil fields have been found on hunches, through precognitive dreams, and by people who didn't know anything about geology," Keeler declared in a 1974 interview. "I had too many incidents that couldn't be explained merely as coincidence."

One survey of Nobel Prize winners in science and medicine found that 72 of 83 Nobel laureates mentioned intuition as being instrumental in their success. Michael Brown, a 1985 Nobel laureate in medicine, ascribed his research team's success to "almost a hand guiding us. We would go from one step to the next, and somehow we would know which was the right way to go, and I really can't tell how we knew that."

Some of us, according to psychological studies, possess a natural gift for predicting the twists and turns of chaotic systems such as the weather and financial markets. In 2001 a British research psychologist gave a group of volunteer subjects a list of eight numbers, telling them these were maximum temperatures for the previous eight days, and asked them to predict the next four numbers. The eight numbers had been generated by a computer and were chaotic sequences, without any obvious patterns. Yet, one quarter of the people tested in the study correctly and consistently predicted the next numbers. Testing for a sensitivity to chaos is being extended to determine if this skill is related to particular personality types, or to an aspect of intelligence like mathematical ability.

"They have some sort of intuition," observes Jeff Pressing, an artificial intelligence professor at Australia's University of Melbourne. "My guess is that they are sensitive to subtle, non-linear structures." As a case in point, Pressing points to some financial traders who make millions of dollars from their trades, but cannot describe their mental process for decision-making. As we will explore in Chapter Five, "The Reach of the Mind," such an aptitude for intuition may in fact spring from a deeper source.

Separating Intuition from Delusion and Obsession

> *"Feeling as though I were delirious with fever, I moved the whole pile of money to the red—and suddenly came to my senses! For the only time in the course of the whole evening, fear laid its icy finger on me and my arms and legs began to shake. With horror I saw and for an instant fully realized what it would mean to me to lose now! My whole life depended on that stake!"*
> —Fyodor Dostoevski, *The Gambler*

Some of you may remember the comedy movie *Groundhog Day*, starring Bill Murray as a television weatherman who wakes up every morning and relives the same day over and over, an endless

repetition of events and character interactions, until he
and starts to transform himself incrementally into a better
This act frees him from being trapped on the treadmill of h own
toxic attitudes and behaviors. This movie was a clever parable for
the themes of reincarnation and karma, the spiritual law of cause
and effect. It also contains valuable cautionary advice about the ob-
sessions and compulsions, inherent in risk-taking, that can degen-
erate good luck into a self-perpetuating streak of misfortune.

When we intentionally engage in attempts to challenge chance,
whether our risk of choice is gambling or the stock market, our
burning desire to win, and the greed that may inspire, can delude
us into discerning order and pattern where there is none. "Sometimes intuition is our inner knowing that we're right, whether we
are or not," is how psychologist David G. Myers frames one of the
dangers we face.

My own experience illustrates what can happen if we fail to separate the whispers of our intuition from the screams of our compulsions. In the aftermath of my eleven-week streak of good luck at
slots, a long period ensued in which I stopped listening to my intuition and plunged into playing the machines with an abandon fueled by greed, envy, and the "gambler's fallacy" of believing another
big win was due. This experience was immensely useful for the research phase of this book, but ended up inflicting damage to my financial well-being.

By referring to the extensive notes I took about my daily playing
practices, attitudes, and experiences, I can identify a single day as
one of the turning points when my good luck flipped into bad. It
was in early May, after my consistent win streak of February into
April, and I had a feeling that a particular dollar slot machine at
Konocti Vista would pay out. I drove to the casino with $100 in my
pocket.

After paying nearly all of my money into the machine, and never
getting more than $10 in return, I became impatient and quit, even
though the feeling persisted that this machine was "pregnant" with
a payout and "due" to birth some jackpots. A young Asian woman
took my place on the stool in front of the machine. As I watched in

astonishment, she almost immediately won a $640 payout. Despite knowing that it wasn't necessarily a jackpot intended for me, that each player's millisecond of difference in play timing determines a win or loss, I silently cursed myself for having given up on the machine too soon. She continued winning on it, up to $160 on almost every pull of the handle, until her husband walked over and convinced her to cash out her impressive winnings.

Feverish and determined now to capitalize on this "hot" machine, I went to the ATM and pulled out another $100 in the form of five twenties. I plopped myself onto the stool, inserted the money, and began punching the "Play" button in an alternating rhythm from fast to slow, counting to ten between each push, to see if I could detect, and then ride, a winning wave. Within fifteen minutes I had fed the machine all five twenties and had won absolutely nothing of substance. My frustration felt volcanic, as if fate had unfairly deprived me of a rightful bounty.

After calming down and summoning my inner observer to provide commentary on the possible lessons of what had transpired, I realized that, while my intuition about the machine had been on target, it simply wasn't my time or my turn to be the recipient of that machine's, or perhaps any machine's, good graces. Sometimes fortune smiles at us. Sometimes fortune laughs at us. How we respond helps shape both our future fortunes and our mental health.

This one experience soon became a pattern of experiences. I couldn't win no matter what strategy I tried. Rather than use a mindfulness practice, in which I would remain present in the moment, feeling for intuitive guidance, I made a decision to allow myself to go on autopilot, mindlessly feeding the machines. I became every casino's dream patron, the one who tries to force luck into submission by will and persistence alone. My thoughts were obsessive and my actions compulsive, and to the extent that I could detach and observe myself, it was an ugly sight to behold.

Most compulsive gamblers, say mental health experts, won early on in their gambling careers and got hooked on the elation and adrenaline of winning. Recent scientific studies have generated findings that can help us understand why we might fall prey to obsessive-compulsive behaviors. Research has shown that our brains are programmed to goad us into continuing to take risks even after a succession of failures, a finding that could help compulsive gamblers, or people prone to taking dangerous risks in the stock market. (Medication has been developed that can help some compulsive gamblers control their habit.)

In a study from the University of Michigan, published in the March 2002 issue of *Science* magazine, six men and six women had the electrical activity in their brains recorded as they played a simple game of chance in which they won or lost money. The specific area of the brain monitored, a part of the medial frontal cortex, is involved in detecting errors, or important negative events. As the test subjects gambled, stronger neural processing signals in this area of the brain occurred when bettors lost more frequently than when they won. One science writer called this electrical crackle of energy "the little devil" that urges us to make reckless decisions when good luck is elusive.

Bettors made more risky choices after suffering a losing streak, a behavior totally absent when they won. "The basic thing we found," reported William Gehring, an assistant professor of psychology, "is that your brain thinks you're due for a win, and it's somehow developing an expectation that after having lost money, you're going to win money." Our brains probably evolved this way, speculated Gehring, "because in the real world there are many cases where a string of bad (luck) will usually be followed by something good."

According to one university study, nearly 16 million Americans may be problem gamblers. Between 1990 and 2001, gambling replaced baseball as the American pastime, and the numbers of Gamblers Anonymous chapters in the U.S. jumped from 650 to 1,500, almost in direct proportion to the explosive growth in the numbers of riverboat and Native American casinos.

"At one end are the disciplined recreational gamblers who play knowing they will lose over time," observed David G. Myers, author of *Intuition: Its Powers and Perils*. "At the continuum's other end are those whose search for phantom riches is fueled by inextinguishable illusions."

To help you determine whether your risk-taking is compulsive, I would urge you to answer the series of gambling questions used by Gamblers Anonymous to detect addicts. That is step one in determining whether the voice you're responding to represents intuition or a type of magical thinking produced by the ego's desire and the brain's compulsive programming.

The Cost of Discounting "Intuition"

Dr. Judith Orloff had been in practice as a psychiatrist for only six months when she had a dream about a client named Christine. On awakening, Orloff had a premonition that Christine would attempt suicide. "This sudden knowledge felt like an arrow hitting the bull's-eye or a chord ringing clear and pure," Orloff wrote in her book, *Second Sight*. "But to be aware of a premonition in the context of being a physician felt alien, threatening. A part of me wanted to deny it, to block it out."

There was no rational basis for Orloff to believe this woman wanted to kill herself; nothing the client said or did had aroused her suspicions. So Orloff ignored the intuitive information. A few days later Christine took an overdose of pills, and the next time Orloff saw her it was in the intensive-care unit of a Los Angeles hospital where she was hooked up to life-support equipment. "By discounting my premonition, I had betrayed both Christine and myself," Orloff confessed. "The only mention of premonitions or other psychic abilities I ever found during my medical education was in textbooks labeling such claims a sign of profound psychological dysfunction."

Orloff says she trained herself to recognize her intuitive voice and separate it from the cacophony of other voices in her mind. She learned what was psychically true by "the sense of rightness that's often present, a clarity, an immediacy, an unconflicted quality so resolute and impartial that the information received isn't open to debate."

In a medical study of sudden infant death syndrome, related by Dr. Melvin Morse in his book *Where God Lives*, nearly twenty-five percent of parents who lost a child to sudden infant death reported having had vivid premonitions of the tragedy days or even hours before it happened. Most of these parents discounted the premonitions, or otherwise failed to act on the information.

We need to know how to distinguish intuition from other mental activity, says psychologist Gail Ferguson, since the accusation is often made that intuitive information "wanders in from nowhere like a stray dog, and that it's easily mistaken for dozens of other normal mental states, such as thought, memory, hope, and fear."

Psychologist Marcia Emery offers this tip for recognizing the appearance of intuition. "When your insight is loud, scary, critical, and full of 'shoulds,' you are in your logical mind." Intuition comes to us effortlessly as wisdom that transcends the normal activity of our minds, and visits us, usually in a whispered voice, as a feeling, a hunch.

Shakti Gawain, in her book *Developing Intuition*, makes a similar distinction: "If there's a part of you feeling that you should take a particular action, that is probably your inner rule-maker or perfectionist, not your intuition. Intuition never guides us with an authoritarian or critical edge. It doesn't impose rules, it never feels heavy-handed or burdensome, it doesn't push us to anything that we're really not ready to do, and it never makes us feel guilty about anything."

Secrets of Lucky People

There are specific ways to distinguish intuition from mind noise. For instance, intuition occurs spontaneously, a sense of knowing that doesn't involve the mental gymnastics of calculating cause and effect. Intuition doesn't come with judgment and shame attached.

Lucky people know how to distinguish intuition from wishful thinking.

If they don't by nature already know how, they learn how by experimenting until they find a technique that works for them.

Here is one proven practice to separate your intuitive voice from the obsessive-compulsive, or the wishful expectations of your ego. "Voice Dialogue" is a process that helps distinguish between the various voices of the mind, the different subpersonalities within us, each with its own distinctive energetic. Developed by psychologists Dr. Hal Stone and Dr. Sidra Stone, and described in their book, *Embracing Our Selves*, it helps us to recognize the voices that come up, such as our internal controller, our critic, our magical child, and dozens of others. This tool can help us understand what parts of self motivate and inspire us, or inhibit and undermine us.

Lucky people know how to quiet their minds to access intuition at will.

Most of us don't know how to access intuitive flashes on a regular basis. Psychologists who have studied this problem have concluded that meditative techniques can help us open this channel. (You will find more on these techniques in Part Three.)

Lucky people are alert to the symptoms in their bodies that herald intuitive messages.

If we are "in our minds" all the time, failing to heed the intelligence reflected through our bodies, we miss out on opportunities to prepare for danger, chance encounters, or even disease and illness within our own bodies.

Lucky people use their intuition, not their logical minds, to decipher the meaning of synchronicity.

Much like our dreams, synchronicities are symbolic. As with

dream work, interpreting meaning in the patterns of coincidence requires the enlistment of our intuition.

Lucky people act on their intuition's guidance even when it doesn't seem to make sense.

Don Browne's story at the beginning of this chapter illustrates the need to treat intuitive information with respect.

"Luck, like intuition," observes Dr. Richard Broughton, a founder of Intuition Laboratories in North Carolina, "may have a psi [psychic] component, which is simply an extrapolation from the growing body of evidence that some individuals can alter the probability of random events to fall in their favor more than chance would predict." Intuitive abilities, lucky streaks, and favorable synchronicities may all indicate that some of us routinely use psi in our daily lives.

CHAPTER 5

The Reach of the Human Mind

"The unthinkable phenomena of ESP appear somewhat less preposterous in the light of the unthinkable propositions of physics."—Arthur Koestler

When the Dallas Cowboys played the Pittsburgh Steelers in the 1996 Super Bowl, I watched the game on television at the home of my former college roommate, Randy Harvey, a sports columnist for the *Los Angeles Times*. A half-dozen other people were present, including another *Times* sports columnist, Mike Downey. At a certain point during the game, as I drifted into a zone of watching the football action without any thoughts, no strategizing, no internal monologue, I suddenly and intuitively knew a Dallas player would intercept the Pittsburgh quarterback's next pass.

"I feel an interception coming," I blurted, loud enough for everyone in the room to hear. On the next play a Dallas defensive back intercepted the pass thrown by the Pittsburgh quarterback, and that turnover became a pivotal play of the game. Several people in the room turned to peer at me in surprise.

"Do you do that often?" Downey inquired.

"It happens sometimes," I replied sheepishly, for some reason feeling embarrassed that I had drawn attention to myself.

Later in the game this feeling came over me again. I knew, without any doubt, that another interception was about to take place. In a lowered voice, so as not to attract more scrutiny, I muttered my prediction. On the next play the same Dallas defender who had intercepted the earlier pass made a second interception, and earned himself a most valuable player award for the game.

Since childhood I have periodically had the experience of accurately predicting pass interceptions in football games, but never fumbles or penalties, or even the outcome of games. These premonitions have always puzzled me. I have feebly attempted to explain the phenomena this way: I feel the onset of interceptions because passing is my favorite part of the game, so I devote more anticipation and excitement to the onset of pass plays. While I don't have a foreshadowing of every interception in every football game, it's also true that each time I can recall experiencing this precognitive sensation, an interception followed less than a minute later.

This intuitive feeling of knowing always comes over me seconds before the interception, a realization that surges into my conscious awareness when my mind is, for lack of a better term, zoned out. My body also responds with an immediate acceleration in my heartbeat and a suddenly fevered forehead, leading up to the flash-heat of elation that momentarily engulfs me once the interception occurs. I have doubts that this skill, at least in my case, can be replicated in a scientific laboratory. It feels like an erratic, uncontrollable aspect of my own peculiar nature. Beyond the simple thrill of experiencing it, I had always questioned, until undertaking the research for this book, whether it had any broader practical value.

"Psychic" is a word that has always made me squeamish. It conjures up the news accounts of "psychic hotlines," staffed by charlatans who have been exposed as preying upon the desperate, the gullible, and the impoverished. It is a word I have long associated with street fortune tellers who tell you they "see" a curse having been placed on you, an evil-eye hex that must be dispelled, and you must come back ten times at $100 a visit so they alone can purify you of this bad luck by burning a candle. Nor did it help soften my aversion to learn that the word "psychic" is equated with psychosis, a deranged state, in American Psychiatric Association literature.

Yet, as I write these words, a memory surfaces of an unusual psychic experience (for lack of a better term) that shook up my rational mind in a profound way. During the summer of 1979 I lived in the Maryland suburbs of Washington, D.C., in an apartment complex known as Westchester Park, consisting of two 18-story high-rise buildings, between which stretched a large swimming pool. On hot and humid afternoons I could often be found sitting beside that pool, reading and writing and daydreaming.

One afternoon I was reclining next to the pool when my thoughts began to drift idly. My gaze swept up the building to my left where I noticed an elderly woman sitting on her ninth-floor balcony, apparently reading a magazine. What initially drew my eyes to her was her bright yellow bathrobe. Due to the distance separating us I couldn't see any details of her face, but I was certain I had never seen the woman before.

For some reason my imagination took over and I began to wonder about this woman, trying to imagine what she had experienced in her life, and whether she had a family, or lived alone. Since I wore sunglasses and sat in the midst of dozens of other people lounging poolside, I felt certain that from such a distance she couldn't possibly know I was even gazing in her general direction. She was the focus of my speculative attentions for no more than two minutes or so before I returned to reading the book in my lap.

Several minutes passed and I glanced up to see that the woman in the bright yellow bathrobe was no longer sitting on her ninth-floor perch. She had descended, taking either stairs or elevator, and now strolled slowly along the sidewalk that led to the swimming pool gate. She entered the pool area, navigated her way through clusters of children, and continued her slow but steady march on shaky, milk-white legs. She seemed to be heading straight toward me. At the foot of my pool chair the elderly lady stopped and stood, hands hooked around the yellow terrycloth of her hips, and silently stared down at me with steel-gray eyes.

"You were using ESP on me, weren't you?" she said in a tone that sounded accusatory.

"No," I found myself beginning to stammer.

"You mentally scanned me," she continued. "You were trying to pick up information. I'm sensitive to these things."

"I don't know what you're talking about," I lied.

She wearily shook her head, obviously disappointed at my attitude. With an audible sigh she turned and walked away, out of the pool area and up the sidewalk, until she disappeared from view into the high-rise building. I don't recall ever seeing this woman again.

Afterwards, my mental process went through all sorts of wild gyrations as I tried to rationalize the incident as nothing more than a chance coincidence. Two strangers had simply thought about each other from a distance at the same time, and one, undoubtedly the more superstitious of the two, had decided to make her fantasy of a connection known to the other. No matter how hard I tried to accept that scenario, it never felt satisfactory, if only because I had never made a practice of fantasizing about a stranger's life before, making coincidence seem even more unlikely as an explanation. At the intuitive level I sensed that a doorway had briefly opened, an alternative to the consensus reality I had always known. It was an opportunity to experience another way of being, and I had reflexively slammed the door shut with my fear of the unknown.

Reflecting on this encounter, I realize how deeply in denial I must have been about my own capacity for paranormal experience. This incident underscores my rational mind's tendency to dismiss or define out of existence every anomaly that I cannot logically explain. In similar fashion, much of the scientific establishment has reflexively clung to the dogma that if prevailing theories about mind and matter can't explain an unusual mind/mind or mind/matter interaction, then the reported anomaly must be a hoax, a misperception, or a fluke with a hidden but prosaic explanation.

The late British novelist and philosopher Arthur Koestler described the schism between rationality and intuition this way: "The study of parapsychology is concerned with two types of events: (a) the results of laboratory experiments, (b) phenomena which occur spontaneously in everyday life. The latter are usually referred to, somewhat contemptuously, as 'anecdotal material,' because the value of such reports depends in most cases on subjective assessments of the reliability of the reporter." Koestler urged scientists to confess that they lack a monopoly on truth about the rules governing the so-called paranormal, and to summon the courage to "admit the existence of levels of reality beyond the vocabulary of rational thought."

Those people who have never been "lucky" enough to experience a "psychic" event cannot really be faulted for doubting such occurrences, any more than we should fault someone blind since birth for doubting the accounts of vivid colors described by someone with sight. Dr. Brugh Joy, a Fellow of the American College of Physicians and author of the 1979 book, *Joy's Way*, framed the issue in a manner that makes sense to me. "While Western science rejects psi phenomena (psi meaning precognition, telepathy, etc.), my personal experience with them has been too extensive and too deep for me to do anything but accept them. . . . How [psi] work and why they work is less important than the direct experience itself. Actually, questions of how and why often impair the natural tendency to have such experiences. I do know that until one experiences it directly, either through another gifted human being or through personal experience, that which is termed 'psi' is only a topic of conversation."

Sigmund Freud, the founder of psychoanalysis, fits Dr. Joy's description of a skeptic whose mind was opened through contact with the experiences of others. Throughout most of his career Freud openly scoffed at claims of telepathy and clairvoyance, and when his brightest student, Carl Jung, embraced those views with his own claims of psychic experiences, Freud ostracized him. Yet, late in his life Freud became convinced that telepathy occurs between analyst and patient, and he speculated that ESP was an archaic method of communication between humans that evolution had demoted with the advent of speech. It is a little known fact that Freud even joined both the British and American Societies for Psychical Research.

Had they still been alive, both Freud and Jung might well have attended the annual meeting of the American Psychoanalytic Association held in Philadelphia in August 2002. During that conference a discussion group of thirty psychoanalysts considered the topic of "Intuition, Unconscious Communication, and Thought Transference." Most of these psychoanalysts had stories to share of telepathic communications and precognitive dreams they had experienced with clients during analysis. "I have found that many scientifically trained people have had an experience along the lines of ESP that they cannot explain. And I have, too," said Dr. Elizabeth Mayer, who chaired the group.

If extrasensory perception does indeed operate periodically in our daily lives, as my own experience and that of others might indicate, many of its effects resemble the condition in life that we call "luck." Those who are skilled at using the "psychic" gift, whether they are consciously aware of it or not, will give the appearance of being lucky people, inordinately blessed by patterns of fortuitous coincidence. To test my suspicions in this regard, I undertook an extensive survey of the experimental research literature in parapsychology, and I sought out scientists and researchers who have devoted their careers to investigating the "margins of reality."

Psi Research: A Brief History of

Scientific investigations of extrasensory perception, those various abilities known to us today as "psi" (pronounced "sigh"), began in a concerted way as an outgrowth of Pulitzer Prize-winning author Upton Sinclair's 1930 book, *Mental Radio*, an account of his wife's extraordinary experiences with ESP and clairvoyance. These experiences attracted the attention of Albert Einstein, the most esteemed scientist of his day, and on May 23, 1930, from his home in Germany, Einstein wrote a preface to Sinclair's book. "In no case," Einstein declared, "should the psychologically interested circles pass over this book heedlessly. . . . The results of the telepathic experiments set forth in this book stand surely far beyond those which a mature investigator holds to be thinkable." Subsequently, Einstein traveled to America and stayed with Mr. and Mrs. Sinclair.

He personally witnessed some of her talents in telepathy and clairvoyance, and in the aftermath he became one of the couple's close,
lifelong friends.

In an introduction to Sinclair's book, Professor William
McDougall, former chairman of the department of psychology at
Oxford University and later head of the department of psychology
at Harvard University, described Mrs. Sinclair as "one of the rare
persons who have telepathic power in a marked degree and perhaps other supernormal powers. The experiments in telepathy
were so remarkably successful as to rank among the very best."

Professor McDougall personally tested Mrs. Sinclair on numerous occasions. The first time he visited the Sinclairs at their home
in Pasadena, California, he informed Mrs. Sinclair that somewhere
in his clothing he carried a picture. He asked her to view it clair-
voyantly and then describe it. Upton Sinclair, who was a witness,
takes up the story: "She sat quietly with her eyes closed and
presently said that she saw a building with stone walls and narrow
windows, and it seemed to be covered with green leaves. Mc-
Dougall took from his inside coat pocket a postcard of one of the
buildings at Oxford, covered with ivy."

After other successful tests of Mrs. Sinclair and a well-known
Los Angeles intuitive, Arthur Ford, Professor McDougall was so intrigued and inspired by the persuasive results that he established a
Department of Parapsychology at Duke University in North
Carolina, dedicated to the study of psi. One of his first assistants
was J. B. Rhine, who, along with his wife, Louisa, both Ph.Ds,
would eventually succeed McDougall as the nation's premier psi researchers.

In her book, *Mind Over Matter*, Professor Louisa Rhine describes
how her husband became interested in the connection between
streaks of gambling luck and psi abilities. It was 1934, and a university student who was visiting Rhine in his office had made a remarkable claim about the gambling skills he used to support
himself financially.

"He had found that he could control the fall of dice—by will power (psychokinesis). At times, he said earnestly, when throwing dice in gambling, he could get the faces of the dice to come up as he wanted them to. He said he could not do it all the time, but only when in a special, highly confident mental state."

Professor Rhine asked the student to demonstrate this ability by throwing dice on his office floor. "His actual success is not on record," Mrs. Rhine reported after her husband's death. "But it was great enough to impress my husband and to arrest his interest and attention so much that it led him to start a new line of inquiry immediately."

In an extensive series of experiments the Rhines asked volunteer test subjects to mentally influence the numbers appearing on several dice as they were thrown. Test subjects either tried to make high combinations appear (eights or higher using two dice) or low combinations of six or less. Dice were either tumbled by hand or tossed by a mechanical device. After nine years of testing, the Rhines found results of psychokinesis in their participants by odds of *one trillion to one* over chance expectation.

As I read through summaries of the huge volume of experimental evidence accumulated by J. B. and Louisa Rhine, I came across this unusual crap-shoot contest held in the early 1940s at Duke University. Four divinity students challenged four skilled crap-shooters to determine which group would be more successful in mentally influencing the roll of dice. The ministerial students prepared for the contest by engaging in group prayer, while the crap-shooters relied on the feeling of luck each had nurtured during years of gambling.

Each participant threw six dice at a time from a cup. After 1,242 throws, the two groups were virtually tied in the scoring. One of the crap-shooters and one of the divinity students scored so far below chance expectation that they significantly lowered their groups' scores. Despite this, the combined results of both groups, reported Louisa Rhine, "would not occur by chance in billions of tests. The result was the highest that had ever been reported over as large a number of runs as this. The divinity students were not se-

ce-throwing ability, but because of their convictions.
prayer may have done, certainly the strong motiva-
tion which the competition induced was effective."

A later experiment determined that people whose thinking is
normally dominated by sensory imagery did better on the die-face
tests when they visualized the desired target face as they threw the
dice. But other researchers in later years paradoxically found evidence that egocentric efforts to will effects to happen were often in-
effective. The reason seemed to be that psi effects are channeled
through the unconscious and not the conscious mind. Most people
identified as "psychic" do not feel personally responsible for their
psi success. Instead, they describe their role as that of a channel, or
a facilitator, for phenomena originating outside themselves.

Further testing conducted at the Rhine laboratory may be of interest to blackjack and poker players. In a series of 85,724 experimental trials over a five-year period, volunteer test subjects were
asked to mentally identify symbols on cards selected and concealed
by the experimenters. These symbols—circles, squares, stars, crosses,
or wavy lines—and five cards bearing each symbol made up a
twenty-five-card deck. Collectively, test subjects accurately guessed
the chosen card symbols at odds better than 100 to 1 against
chance. A man named Hubert Pearce, for example, had an uncanny
accuracy at card-guessing that exceeded chance expectation by
odds of *8 million million million to one*!

"The findings of ESP and PK (psychokinesis) certainly have a
definite bearing on the luck an individual will have in winning and
in losing," concluded Louisa Rhine. "With PK and the rules that
govern it, the good and bad luck streaks are no longer so unex-
plainable as they have seemed."

A key question became whether test subjects in the Rhine experiments were using telepathy, clairvoyance, or precognition. Did
they read the researcher's mind (telepathy) for the correct card? Did
they mentally "see" the correct card (clairvoyance)? Or did they
"read" the future (precognition) to discern the card that would be
chosen?

To test precognition and its uses in gambling, people who had performed effectively on previous precognition tests at the Rhine laboratory were recruited to try to intuitively predict a series of roulette wheel spins (for red and for black) at a specific casino on a specific date. These predictions were then combined, based on common patterns, to produce a list of bets according to consensus. With this list in hand the researchers went to the casino and began betting whenever they observed thirteen or more hits in twenty-five spins of the roulette wheel. Using this method they won a lot of money, so they claimed, and later used this method of precognitive consensus with success in playing craps and baccarat.

As you might imagine, these results from the Rhine laboratory, being so extraordinary yet having failed to offer an energy-transfer mechanism to show how the effects took place, attracted a storm of dismissive criticism and disbelief from most of the scientific establishment. Probability theory expert Warren Weaver, former professor of mathematics at the University of Wisconsin, voiced the concerns of many when he wrote of the Rhine data: "I find this a subject that is so intellectually uncomfortable as to be almost painful. . . . We are asked to accept an interpretation that destroys the most fundamental ideas and principles on which modern science has been based; we are asked to give up the irreversibility of time, to accept an effect that shows no decay with distance and hence involves 'communication' without energy being involved."

Yet, Professor Weaver, after examining some of the data, expressed "complete confidence in the scientific competence and personal integrity of Professor (J. B.) Rhine." Weaver went on to state: "I cannot explain away Professor Rhine's evidence. . . . In any very long probability experiment there will occur highly remarkable runs of luck . . . but I know of no analysis of Rhine data, based on such considerations, that makes it reasonable to believe that their success can be explained in this way."

Over the years other researchers validated some aspects of the Rhine work, particularly a phenomenon that came to be known as the "decline effect." Most test subjects who started the experiments by showing strong psi abilities, had, with repeated testing, shown less success, an effect some experimenters attribute to fatigue or om. Probability theorists countered that such a decline was pr⸌ ⸍ctable because it demonstrated one of the laws of probability—that over time any unusual deviation from chance expectation will return to the mean average.

But to the Rhines and other psi scientists, this decline pattern was more evidence for psi effects because it helped refute the claims of some critics that positive psi results were due to recording errors, flawed experimental procedures, or dice abnormalities. "If any such distorting elements had been present, they would be expected to remain constant," pointed out Norma Bowles and Fran Hynds, author of the 1978 book, *Psi Search*. "Since the results fluctuated in a way that indicated the presence of the decline effect, only psi remained as the factor responsible for the experimental results."

The effects of attitude and atmosphere on our likelihood of success in both gambling and parapsychological experiments are, apparently not coincidentally, identical. Those attitudes, observed Louisa Rhine, are "characterized as relaxed, and almost playful in contrast to the negative ones of tension and anxiety. Better results are secured by those who consider themselves lucky than those who think they are unlucky."

Based on my observation, the often frustrated attitude many people display while gambling, and the distractive atmosphere most of us experience in gambling casinos, doesn't exactly invite psi to emerge and conspire with luck for our benefit. Dr. Dean Radin suspects that the noise, smells, and visually distracting conditions stifle psi. Yet, he also understands that "many gambling games are essentially identical to psi experiments conducted in the laboratory."

While associated with the University of Nevada in 1995, Dr. Radin obtained four years' worth of daily payout data from the Continental Casino in Las Vegas, thanks to a casino executive who was curious whether any patterns of psi effects could be discerned from this information. After analyzing the player winnings data, he noticed that four of the six biggest slot machine jackpots over the previous four years occurred within a day of the full moon. The most unexpected finding came when he compared the daily payout rates—money actually won by gamblers each day—to the lunar cycles. Gamblers averaged two percent higher payouts during the full moon.

A dozen other studies have produced evidence that on days when the earth's geomagnetic field is quiet, psi performance generally improves. By comparing the daily payout rates from the Continental Casino to records of geomagnetic fluctuations, Radin also found a correlation—payout rates were generally lower when geomagnetic activity was higher. Somehow, it seemed, geomagnetic activity repressed gambler's luck.

Speculation about why this happens began to center on an area of the human brain approximating the so-called mystical "third eye" in the forehead, where tiny deposits of magnetic materials have been found. These magnetite fragments have been theorized to be vestiges of an early evolutionary navigation ability in humans—one still possessed by birds, turtles, and other creatures, which have been found to have magnetite in their heads. Perhaps the magnetite in our foreheads goes screwy during geomagnetic fluctuations and interferes with psi functioning. Maybe the magnetite somehow directly facilitates the functioning of psi. These speculations give me pause to wonder whether some people truly do, quite literally, attract luck to themselves as if they were magnets.

Psi: The Link to Luck and Intuition

In another of his extraordinary experiments, Dr. Radin decided to test the question of whether "some cases of remarkable luck, sometimes attributed to 'intuitive hunches,' may be due to gaining information about future events, specifically emotional responses to future events, as slot machine jackpots are likely to induce."

He designed an experiment to monitor the unconscious responses of autonomic nervous systems to future events, and test the observation that a "great majority of spontaneous psi experiences, including runs of remarkable luck, are associated with strong emotions." By monitoring test participants' heart rate, fingertip blood volume, and skin conductance level before, during, and after they were shown randomly selected pictures depicting either emotional or calming scenes, Radin hoped to detect unconscious psi perception. These changes in their nervous systems, if psi was at work in this way, would occur *before* they visually saw the pictures.

Volunteers totaling twenty-three men and twenty-seven women were recruited, most from the University of Nevada. From April 1996 through March 1997, these test subjects were seated in front of a computer screen one at a time and hooked up to the monitoring devices. The participant pressed a mouse button and a colorful picture appeared on the screen for three seconds followed by a blank screen for ten seconds. The participant then pressed the button to display another picture. All together, 150 randomly selected images were used—one hundred calm pictures of trees or animals, and fifty pictures portraying erotic or violent subject matter.

What Radin discovered lends support to my own experience of heart rate changes and heat sensations seconds before those exciting football passes were intercepted. Of his fifty test subjects, thirty-two showed persistent changes in their autonomic nervous systems seconds *before* seeing the emotional imagery, but not before viewing the calming pictures. Their bodies unconsciously responded to future emotional events. The experiment proved to be an extraordinary demonstration of how precognition is felt in the body first, much as people describe feeling "hunches" or a visceral sense of "knowing" before their conscious minds process any information.

"Presentiment" is the term Radin coined for this unconscious form of psi perception that is a response to future emotional events. He eventually did three followup experiments that also demonstrated the physiological evidence of how, in his words, "many people literally get a gut feeling before something bad happens."

A rudimentary version of Radin's experiments produced similar results as far back as 1962 in tests at New Jersey's Newark College of Engineering. A professor of Industrial Engineering, John Mihalasky, was hooked up to a device measuring blood volume in one of his fingers. His associate, Douglas Dean, sat in another room and concentrated for twenty seconds on the names of people Mihalasky did and didn't know. When Dean mentally sent names important to Mihalasky, striking dips occurred in the blood volume of his finger. Mihalasky allegedly reacted to eighty percent of Dean's transmissions as recorded by blood volume dips.

As the two men reported in their 1974 book, *Executive ESP*, "Mihalasky's biggest unconscious reactions were to the mental transmissions of the name of his daughter, and to the name of an associate who was putting a great deal of pressure on him." Dean commented how their experimental results "seemed to indicate that people are especially sensitive at the bio-communication level to any stimuli that has a direct relation to their own well-being."

All of these rather startling findings got support from an unexpected quarter in 1997 with publication of an article in *Science* magazine based on an experiment by four neuroscientists. They measured skin conductance in ten normal people, and in six patients with brain damage, as they all played a card game for money using four decks of cards. Two of the decks had been stacked, unbeknownst to the players, with a high percentage of losing cards. Amazingly, both the normal and the brain-damaged people showed a big jump in skin conductance response when they unknowingly selected cards from the high-loss decks, but not when they selected from the unstacked decks. It was as if their nervous systems provided an early warning for high risk.

Not only that, but the test subjects with normal brains, in the researcher's words, "began to generate anticipatory skin conductance responses whenever they pondered a choice that turned out to be risky, before they knew explicitly that it was a risky choice." What did the four scientists make of these results? They were so perplexed (and so reluctant to venture into the parapsychological realm of explanations), they could only offer a guess that some previously unidentified addition to the mechanism of human reasoning had been uncovered by the experiment.

One of the four neuroscientists, Antonio Damasio, wrote a book in 1994, *Descartes' Error*, in which he used results from experimental neuroscience to make a persuasive case that the human emotional system, rather than being an example of the brain's most primitive evolutionary functions, is an important part of a human being's "higher" rational self and important to decision-making. Parapsychology researcher Dr. Richard Broughton extrapolates from this that "the emotional system, as outlined by Damasio, is an integrated system that happens to cover most of the ESP responses. It is capable of generating emotional body states such as the feelings that play a part in psychic intuitive experiences."

Dr. Broughton considers psi abilities to be a product of human evolution, and as such, "we must remember that evolution is an extremely economical process. Evolution is not inclined to build entirely new systems, but instead it adapts existing systems to serve new functions. The way ESP gets its job done is likely to be in the form of an 'add on' to some existing system." The "presentiment" studies conducted by Radin and others suggest to Broughton that "our emotions play a role in processing ESP information." He points out that even the Greek roots of the word "telepathy" translate into "feeling at a distance," once again suggesting a link between our emotional systems and psychic phenomena.

Inside A Slot Machine's "Consciousness"

We are standing in a casino, you and I—any casino will do—and we are about to play a slot machine. Again, for our purposes any machine will work, but for the sake of familiarity let's play a three-reel quarter machine, one of those "sizzling sevens" with a 1,000-coin jackpot payout. Even before we drop the three quarter maximum bet into this machine, it is already engaged in play action, sorting through an unending stream of winning and losing numbers, even though from our vantage point the reels with symbols aren't moving and nothing seems to be happening.

Here is a short and simple description of the process that is invisible to us. The "brain" of the slot machine is a microchip with random number generator programming, and whether the machine is being played or not, every second this microchip generates *up to one thousand* number combinations corresponding to symbols on the three reels adorning the "face" of the slot machine. After inserting our money, the instant we press the "Play" button or pull the slot machine's arm, one of the set of numbers flashing in the machine's "consciousness" is grabbed and reproduced as symbols for us that are then translated into either winning or losing money.

How does a random number generator work? What kind of winning payout formula is programmed onto the microchip inside slot machines? Is there a concern, a legitimate one, among casinos or slot machine manufacturers that psychically gifted people might be able to influence the machines? To learn answers to these and other questions, I contacted the world's largest maker of slot machines, International Game Technology, headquartered in Reno, Nevada. This company produces seventy percent of the slot machines sold in the United States, and fifty percent of the machines sold worldwide. IGT's director of public relations, Rick Sorensen, arranged for me to interview the software engineer in charge of random number generators, James Vasquez, IGT's director of firmware engineering.

Vasquez suggested that if we want to visualize what is happening inside a slot machine on the random number generator, we should think of a computer screen. Running down the screen is a stream of numbers, one thousand every second, flying by so fast we can't visually identify any single one. The screen is a streaming mass of gray. Whenever we press the "Play" button to initiate a game, some of those numbers are selected. I think of this process using a wind tunnel metaphor. Billions of numbers are blowing around inside a wind tunnel, and you press the button activating an invisible hand that reaches in and snatches three numbers, one for each reel of symbols on the machine. Each number for each reel corresponds to one of sixty-four possible symbols on that reel.

"On a three-reel slot machine the number pulled for the first reel has no influence on the numbers of the second or third reels," Vasquez told me. He explained that the random number generators

used by IGT are designed to function for up to forty years, well beyond the life of the slot machine itself, before the number sequences would begin repeating.

Statistical payback percentages, the amount of money returned
to players over time, are determined by each casino for each individual machine. Vasquez described how the payback percentages
are calculated. "We offer, maybe for the same game, nine payout
schedules for it, and the casino chooses the one they want. Every
casino has its own ideas about whether slots should be looser (higher
payouts) to get more play, or tighter, with some casinos having the
attitude that these people are coming no matter what, and we can
run the machines tighter and make more money. A lot of that decision hinges on demographics, where you're at in the nation.
Competition plays a large role in what payback percentages casinos
select. In order to give them that wide variety of choices, we give
them a chip they can put in and change the payback percentage.
But this has nothing to do with the random number generator. That
is a separate chip.

"To illustrate statistical payback percentages, I have pulled up
one of our slot pay tables. I don't know which game it is. After a
thousand handle pulls, the payout percentage could be as low as 50
percent, and the upper percentage could be as high as 140 percent.
We put confidence ranges in so we can tell casinos we're 90 percent
confident that after a thousand plays you'll be paying out between
50 percent and 140 percent. As you go to ten thousand pulls, now
that number is between 77 percent and 99.8 percent. As you continue to go on it converges down to the payback percentage the
casino has selected. Some of these games may take upwards of a
million handle pulls and still be swinging by as much as four or five
percent. If the casino is making a 98 percent payback promise to
players, even after a million handle pulls it's still statistically likely
the machine could be paying back 101 percent, and that would be
within our confidence ranges that the pay table is functioning correctly."

When I mentioned parapsychological research with random

number generators, the attempts to measure mental effects on number outputs, Vasquez professed to be uninformed. He did indicate that IGT tries to ensure the randomness of its random number chips by taking thousands of samples and conducting a battery of tests. "When it comes to influencing random number generators," he said, "I am not aware of any real way to do it."

Let's say a slot machine is "hot," paying out in the 140 percent range, or $1.40 being returned for every dollar played into it. Does the casino know from one day to the next when a particular machine is on a hot streak? "Oh yeah, they do," replied Vasquez. "Every slot machine in a casino these days is connected to some sort of central computing system that can tell how much coin has been played and how much was won. It's done for taxation reasons, too."

That being the case, the most closely guarded secret a casino has each day must be the list of slot machines that are hot. Anyone who discovers, or intuits, a hot machine, and plays out the streak, certainly qualifies as a lucky person. When I shared this revelation with a friend, he only half-jokingly suggested that maybe some lucky slot players are "reading the minds" of those casino executives who know the placement and payout schedules of hot machines.

A Psi Ghost in the (Slot) Machine

Let's imagine for a moment that we can slowwwwww down the passage of time until the numbers percolating in the random number generator, normally being spewed out at one thousand per second, are instead popping up one per second. Let's also assume we have a counter that provides a readout showing the stream of numbers per minute. If we had the formula of which numbers correspond to which symbols on the slot machine reels, we could decipher favorable trends in the number stream that would make us lucky. That's one way to visualize how psi could work to the advanage of slot players. Let's examine what decades of research evidence shows about whether human consciousness can interact with random number generators.

German physicist Helmut Schmidt, while a scientist for the Boeing Company Laboratory, invented the random number generator (RNG) in 1969 to conduct a series of dice-throwing experiments. His RNG device contained a small amount of strontium 90, a radioactive substance whose subatomic particles deteriorate randomly. Each decaying particle generated an electrical signal reflected on the RNG's counter as either a 1 or a 2 position. Test subjects were asked to exert control over the counter by concentrating their attention on a circle of small light bulbs corresponding to the machine's internal counter positions.

Many test subjects in separate trials demonstrated an ability to will the lights to move in clockwise or counter-clockwise directions. Schmidt's experimental results with RNGs exceeded chance expectation by odds of over *10,000 to 1*. After years of study, Schmidt could never decide if his subjects were affecting movement of the lights directly, or if they were mentally influencing the rate of strontium 90 decay and, in turn, affecting the RNGs' binary number sequences.

Other RNG experimenters added new levels of sophistication to the research process. Beginning in 1979, physicist Robert G. Jahn, former Dean of the Princeton University School of Engineering, and clinical psychologist Brenda J. Dunne produced an impressive body of evidence demonstrating how the human mind could affect the functions of computers. They called the program that they helped establish the Princeton Engineering Anomalies Research (PEAR), dedicated to applying the techniques of modern engineering science to a systematic study of human consciousness-related anomalies.

They experimented with their own version of an RNG, which they called a random event generator. Here is their description from *Margins Of Reality*, a book Jahn and Dunne co-authored: "Such machines are based on a source of electronic 'white noise' generated by some random microscopic physical process, such as a thermal electron current in a solid-state diode, a gaseous discharge, or a radioactive decay. Electronic logic circuitry then transforms this noise into a regularly spaced string of random alternating binary pulses, or 'bits' (for example: +,-,+,-,-,+,+) that subsequent circuitry then counts, displays, and records."

Test subjects were seated near the machine and asked to mentally influence its binary output, by coaxing the RNGs to produce either larger-than-average or smaller-than-average sequences of numbers. Some subjects engaged in meditation or visualization techniques prior to testing, while others simply used their natural competitiveness to try and better their own results or outperform others participating in the experiment. Many subjects treated the computers as if they were human and tried strategies of coaxing, begging, or even threats to achieve their desired results. (Though I wasn't present, I can imagine the sort of verbal onslaught the computers must have been subjected to: "Come on, resonate with me!" . . . "Please, unless you cooperate, I won't get any supper!" . . . "Damn you, boy, do what I say or I'll unplug you!")

Tactics that seemed to work well at times for some subjects usually ended up being inconsistent and only fleetingly effective. "The most effective operators seem to associate successful performance with the attainment of some sense of 'resonance' with the device," Jahn and Dunne concluded. One test subject described the connection he felt with the random event generator as "a state of immersion in the process which leads to a loss of awareness of myself and the immediate surroundings." Another participant reported: "I don't feel any direct control over the device, more like a marginal influence when I'm in resonance with the machine. It's like being in a canoe; when it goes where I want, I flow with it."

These references to "resonance" and a "loss of awareness" of self and surroundings echo precisely the words and phrases I used to describe my experience with the slot machines during my own streak of luck. Jahn and Dunne discovered, after years of experimentation, that "consciousness, through intention, can marginally influence its physical reality to a degree dependent on its subjective resonance with the system or process."

What I also sensed for myself in relation to slot machines is that my unconscious mind had to be like an open channel, free of internal noise and external distraction, for "luck" to occur. This seems to be equally true for achieving psi success in a laboratory. Our normal ego processes seem to inhibit our use of psi because the ego self-consciously reduces spontaneity. As our ego tries to analyze and to define our experience in the moment, it automatically limits our capacity for experience. As Jahn and Dunne observe, "Unconscious or subconscious expectations or aversions play at least as important a role as conscious intention in determining the effects."

Some of the Princeton project test subjects displayed a phenomenal ability to affect the patterns of random bits being generated by the computers. One subject, whose identity was undisclosed, completed 100 experimental tests over a several-year period, producing results that Jahn and Dunne hailed as having occurred with "such a low likelihood of chance" that the chance factor was nonexistent.

Nearly a half-million experimental trials were eventually carried out at Princeton, demonstrating the ability of the human mind to slightly skew the output of random number generators and nudge outcomes in desired directions. "Gamblers throughout history have believed that they could affect the outcome of a random process like rolling dice or shuffling cards," commented Dunne in 1992. "The phenomenon we're measuring is a lot more subtle, but it's the same idea and we've measured it in the laboratory."

Experiments in 1986 at Stanford Research Institute (SRI), directed by Dr. Edwin May, concluded that the effects observed in RNGs weren't caused by psychokinesis (the act of moving objects, or in this case numbers, with mind force). The test subjects seemed to be using precognition in determining the exact moment to play. SRI used a pseudo-random-number generator that produced a long sequence of seemingly random numbers (taken from a seed number in a mathematical formula), and in this sense these RNGs were similar to the ones used in nearly all modern slot machines.

Dr. Richard Broughton describes the experiment this way: "To succeed in the test, the subject had to press the key at the right moment to 'grab' a good seed number as they flew by," which involved making a "prediction within a very tight window—20 milliseconds, to be precise. The idea that a person could predict when to initiate the muscular movements that will result in a key press at precisely the right 20-millisecond moment seems absolutely mind-boggling. Yet that is what the SRI experiment demonstrated." Dr. May and his co-researcher on the project, Dr. Dean Radin, coined the term "intuitive data sorting" to refer to this ability to press the key at the most advantageous instant to capture the most desirable sequence of numbers.

Other experimenters in Europe were obtaining equally impressive results from some of their test subjects. In Holland, at the University of Amsterdam, fourteen persons were tested in 1996 for their ability to influence a random number generator, and three exhibited an ability to mentally affect the number streams to such a degree that the scientists testing them matter-of-factly declared that "paranormal effects have been obtained in this experiment."

In a May 2000 issue of *Physics World*, a professional journal for physicists, a report appeared about a physicist at the University of Athens in Greece who had done an analysis of findings from RNG experiments in Germany. The scientist had verified the accuracy of German claims that some people could mentally influence the statistical distribution of random bits of data on a microchip. This evidence appeared to suggest, commented *Physics World*, "that the mind could weakly sustain the 'direction' of any naturally occurring localized deviations from chance, such as a run. . . . The operator could affect the patterns by which the bits are arranged in time, even though their average value remained unchanged."

The cumulative impact of all these various RNG studies over several decades has been to create a virtually unassailable body of evidence. A meta-analysis of 597 RNG experiments was conducted by two researchers using sixteen study quality measures for control. (A meta-analysis is a statistical technique, common in the behavioral sciences and medicine, in which experimental results from numerous studies are brought together and analyzed to reveal patterns and the overall validity of data.)

This meta-analysis found an enormous overall indication of

"mind over matter" effects. To nullify the overall positive results of these studies, another *54,000 experiments* would have to be conducted showing no evidence of psi in RNG performance to reduce the mound of evidence back down to an overall chance level.

Group-Mind Effects and Precognition

On that day of infamy, September 11, 2001, when most people on the planet were absorbed by news accounts of the terrorist attacks on New York and Washington, D.C., thirty-seven computers scattered around the world—from Switzerland to India to Brazil—were using random-number-generating microchips to electronically "flip" virtual coins. The Global Consciousness Project, as it's called, seeks to determine if events which become the focal point of humankind's collective thought can affect the usual randomness of these virtual coin tosses.

A large statistical spike in the second-by-second data stream for the thirty-seven computers occurred from the hour the first plane hit the World Trade Center until the end of the day on September 11, an effect far beyond chance or coincidental occurrence. Similar spikes in the data had been recorded on other dramatic days when world attention had been focused, such as the funeral of Princess Diana and the sinking of Russia's *Kursk* nuclear submarine.

Dr. Dean Radin characterized these data spikes as "the level of surprise associated with an observed deviation of the RNG outputs from chance expectation. To cause those spikes the RNGs have to repeatedly produce either too many 0s or too many 1s than they 'should' by chance. Another way of describing this is that the patterns being produced by the RNGs were more orderly than could be expected by sheer dumb luck."

Computer expert Richard Shoup, formerly a scientist with the Xerox Corporation, did an analysis of the 9/11 data in a study for the Boundary Institute, and concluded: "This single day (September 11) can be uniquely and readily distinguished by statistical variance and correlations of the RNGs from any other day in the four-month period examined."

In the 9/11 data collected by the thirty-seven computers across the planet, Shoup found three baffling effects. A one-second anomaly in the data occurred during the terrorist attacks on the World Trade Center, as the images of the disaster-in-progress were being beamed through televisions worldwide. Second, at around 5:30 A.M. Eastern Daylight Time on the morning of September 11, a half-hour duration spike in the computer data stream occurred, an anomaly with odds Shoup estimated to be thousands to one. "No similar deviations were seen in four surrounding months of data," wrote Shoup. "We have no immediate explanation for the provocative fact that this anomaly *preceded* the primary events of Sept. 11 by over three hours." Lastly, in principle the thirty-seven RNGs are all independent, with no interaction between them. Yet, "a significant correlation among the RNGs and a dramatic increase in variance occurred early in the morning on Sept. 11 and continued throughout the day."

What accounts for these reported effects? Professor Roger Nelson of the Princeton University Engineering Anomalies Research program, who directs the Global Consciousness Project, notes that "an unusual coherence of thought and feeling" on the part of a large segment of global humanity does seem to affect the subatomic level of reality. Other scientists who studied the data have drawn a link between the human brain as an electrical device and its possible influence on magnetic fields and electrical equipment. "It appears that consciousness may sometimes produce something that resembles, at least metaphorically, a nonlocal field of meaningful information," read a notice posted on the project's Web site.

Richard Shoup advanced three possible classes of explanations for the observed RNG effects:

(1) "Somehow the combined effects of many people thinking similar thoughts causes changes in the fundamental parameters of physical devices."

(2)   Some sort of field was "generated or affected by the events of 9/11 and this field in turn affects the fundamental randomness of certain devices all over the world."

(3)   RNGs don't simply give us information, "but are affected backwards in time from observers and other events."

The Princeton University research team has examined the impact of group consciousness on streams of information in a variety of group settings. They placed portable random event generators in professional meetings, in the midst of religious rituals, and among meditators during consciousness workshops. What they found mirrored the results of previous experiments with individuals. "High degrees of attention, intellectual cohesiveness, shared emotion, or other coherent qualities of the groups tend to correlate with the statistically unusual deviations from theoretical expectation." In other words, the energetic focus of attention by individuals or groups can, both consciously and unconsciously, have the effect of influencing or ordering otherwise random flows of information.

Perhaps human minds generate consciousness fields and these fields can interact with the informational level of reality within the "consciousness" of computers. (For more psi theories, refer to Appendix A.) Dr. Radin of the Institute for Noetic Sciences in Northern California elaborated on this theory in an interview with me. "Albert Einstein said God doesn't play dice with the universe. So if he's right, then maybe there are causes for things which appear to be random. People usually think of mind-over-matter as the mind pushing matter around. After many years of looking we've never found anything that is causal in that form. Since we do get positive results in these experiments, it's more likely that what we are dealing with is the relationship between mind, matter, and information. The mind, in a sense, is an information-generating and -processing machine. There are informational ways of describing matter, and vice versa.

"Psychokinesis (PK) and precognition can look the same. We see this in the lab all the time. Because the PK and precognitive outcomes are so similar, many of my colleagues are beginning to think that they are really the same thing seen from different directions. Maybe they are part of a fundamental process having to do with the direction in which information flows. For example, when you talk on a cell phone there are extremely small amounts of energy being used. If you were speaking to somebody and they said something mundane, it would have little or no effect on you. But if they said to you, 'I'm giving you one million dollars,' it would have a huge effect. The only difference was the information. If we are able to be in communion informationally with a device, such as a RNG or a slot machine, the effect could look like a gigantic force, but in fact was no force at all."

Remote Viewing for Riches

Clairvoyance ("clear seeing") is information received from a distant or unknown location, beyond the reach of our ordinary senses. It has become synonymous with the term "remote viewing," which represents a more scientific way to describe "astral projection,"a term from the lexicon of New Age beliefs. One way for us to think of remote viewing, in the words of psychologist Dr. David Loye, is "a wireless kind of 'television' existing within the unconscious minds of most of us."

Many attempts have been made, both in gambling and investing, to translate remote viewing skills into winning money. Starting in the mid-1970s, laser physicist Dr. Hal Puthoff, his wife, and their friends made repeated trips to Las Vegas casinos and played the roulette wheels based on a remote viewing strategy Puthoff had developed. Prior to playing, while still in their hotel room, they used visualization to try and guess ten or so spins of the wheel in advance, calculating those spins from the point the roulette ball would land on a green 00 marker. Once in the casino and standing at the roulette table, they waited until the green 00 marker came up, and then placed bets according to their predictions. Puthoff claims they generally always won back the cost of their trip and a profit on top of that.

During the mid-1980s, physicist Russell Targ and Keith Harary, a Long Island-born remote viewer in his early thirties, used "associative" remote viewing to play the silver futures market. Their technique, as described by Jim Schnabel in his book, *Remote Viewing: The Secret History of America's Psychic Spies*, operated like this: "On a Sunday, from a pool of several dozen Bay Area target sites, Targ would select two. One—say, the dramatic Transamerica skyscraper in San Francisco—would signify 'market up on Monday,' The other—say, Fisherman's Wharf—would signify 'market down on Monday.' Harary would not know about either of these sites. He would simply be asked to remote-view, precognitively, the site to which Targ would take him the following afternoon, after the market had closed. Targ, of course, would take him to the site—either Fisherman's Wharf or the Transamerica building—that corresponded to the market's movement."

"It started as an experiment," Schnabel reports, "but after Harary had made two successful predictions of the daily market for a particular silver-futures option, an investor jumped in, betting real money, and Harary had seven more hits." After a period of weeks, though, Targ and Harary had a personal falling-out that culminated in a lawsuit, their investor bolted, and this particular precognitive money-generating scheme came to an abrupt end. Hal Puthoff also used a similar remote-viewing protocol in a silver-futures investment scheme that he capitalized on to save a private school from bankruptcy. He reportedly trained several of the school board members in associative remote viewing, sending their buy or sell orders to his broker, and in a month allegedly cleared the $25,000 needed so that the school near his home in Menlo Park could stay open.

Schnabel concluded: "The data suggested that remote viewers tended to see the probable future rather than the actual future; perhaps this explained why lottery numbers and other low-probability targets were so hard to precognize."

Statistician Jessica Utts evaluated CIA-sponsored remote-viewing experiments done at Stanford Research Institute and at Science Applications International Corporation. She found that even though "only about one percent of those who volunteered to be tested were consistently successful," their phenomenal test results indicated to her that "remote viewing is an ability that differs across individuals, much like athletic ability or musical talent." Additionally, she uncovered "compelling evidence" in the data that precognition, "in which the target is selected after the subject has given the description, is also successful." Utts couldn't avoid the conclusion that perhaps humans "do have a psychic sense, much like our other senses, and that it works by scanning the future for possibilities of major change much as our eyes scan the environment for visual change and our ears are responsive to auditory change."

Psychologist Ray Hyman, a professional critic of psi research, and a member of the Committee for the Scientific Investigation of Claims of the Paranormal, examined the same data as Utts, and though he disagreed with her on some points, he still confessed: "The case for psychic functioning seems better than it ever has been. . . . I have to admit that I do not have a ready explanation for these observed effects."

What Is "the Zone"?

Being in "the zone" is a state of mind recognized, if not experienced, by most athletes. In 1986 *The New York Times* quoted a professional tennis player describing the zone as "so complete and intense that it evokes a state of almost semiconscious euphoria— one that many believe bears a resemblance to hypnosis."

"Peak experience" is the term coined by the late psychologist Abraham Maslow to describe this state of mind. He called it "profound moments of understanding or rapture" when a person feels harmony with life and the cosmos, and feels a sense of having transcended ordinary consciousness.

Former *Washington Post* reporter Chip Brown, in his book about alternative healing, *Afterwards, You're a Genius*, describes the zone this way: "Heart surgeons, clairvoyants, gamblers—all performers, really—acknowledge the concept of the zone, of getting into a rhythm, of feeling that time can be slowed or speeded up as needed, that outcomes can be anticipated and failure is not possible. . . . Moving objects or imparting information (with the mind) might not be a matter of bending reality to your will but of participation in it, of meshing with it as you would flow along with a partner in a dance."

British psychologist Stan Gooch has detailed his experiences at both "routine" gambling, as he calls it, and "paranormal" gambling within the zone. To him being in the zone "involves intuitive judgments not only of how to bet, but when to bet. I must never plan to bet. It must be through intuitive impulse." When "indicators" appear, he seizes the opportunity to gamble. These indicators vary, ranging from synchronicities to precognitive hunches. They are peculiar to Gooch, but during my own eleven-week lucky streak I found they worked for me as well. "Like most gamblers," Gooch relates, "I still sometimes gamble compulsively, out of depression or boredom. On such occasions I then face much the same odds as everyone else."

Entering the zone can also be a group experience with luck effects that have paranormal implications. One night at the end of Chip Brown's research trip to Las Vegas, where he had been interviewing parapsychological researchers, he went to Bally's casino and witnessed the zone manifest at a roulette wheel. He watched a man from New York bet the number 17 and lose until, finally, in exasperation, he cried out to no one in particular, "I can't believe 17 hasn't come up." In a dramatic flourish the man pushed a giant stack of chips onto 17 red, and Brown, along with five other players at the table, got into the spirit and also stacked their chips onto that number. Collectively, their entire focus, their intention, their energetic presence, was directed at willing and wishing that number and color to appear.

Brown relates what happened next. "Everyone at the table who had been pursuing separate strategies all night was suddenly bound together, pulling as one . . . projecting our intention." The roulette wheel began spinning and the metal ball whirled, and out it popped, to settle on . . . number 17 red! Brown and his fellow gamblers released a roar "that rocked the far ends of the casino." He goes on to speculate about whether this was merely a fortuitous coincidence. "If I had to take an official position, I would say the number just came up; it was gorgeous dumb luck. Off the record, I like to think maybe not. I conceal the hope that something unexplained happened, and that we all contributed to it."

Extrasensory Luck

Some behavioral attitudes and practices have emerged from parapsychological research to help predict whether you might perform well in a psi experiment, and by extension be capable of using psi in your everyday life. You may recall a term used earlier in this book, meta-analysis, a statistical tool used to combine data from numerous similar experiments. Cornell University psychology professor Daryl Bem and a colleague conducted a meta-analysis of twenty-five experiments on telepathy conducted between 1945 and 1981, and published their results in a 1994 issue of *Psychological Bulletin*.

They found people who scored high on psi tests "were more likely to have scored high on emotional and perceptual orientation indices, to be artistically creative or possibly extroverted, to have had previous ESP-like experiences, or to have had previously studied a mental discipline like meditation." From this data Professor Bem detected evidence that humans receive psi information as a weak signal that is normally masked by both internal and external sensory noise. Practices like meditation help to induce "psi-conducive states" that reduce this sensory noise and thus magnify the signal.

As a general rule, here are some of the other attributes and ways of being that seem instrumental in helping to determine whether your psi proficiency and luck are wedded.

Lucky people know how to quiet their minds, how to be positive, relaxed, and playful, and how to project confidence about being successful.

It does appear to be true that people who believe they are lucky—not pretend to be, but in their hearts truly believe it—usually perform better on psi tests and utilize that belief in their lives to manifest even more luck.

Lucky people can detach from their egos and their most cherished beliefs long enough to accept and absorb the lessons of "psychic" experiences.

As with learning to trust their intuition, a lucky person learns to accept the possibility that other levels of reality exist, and to surrender to the prospect that the rational mind may never be able to provide satisfactory answers.

Lucky people know how to enter the zone at will, or they can sense the physical and emotional cues of its approach.

Because emotions play an important role in processing "psychic" information, lucky people are in touch with their feelings, and able to express emotions in healthy ways that enhance their well-being.

CHAPTER 6

Tapping the Predictive Power of Your Dreams

"A dream uninterpreted is like a letter unopened."
—Jewish proverb.

"Human minds, when set free by sleep, or in detached states of excited derangement, perceive things which minds involved with the body cannot see."—Marcus Tullius Cicero (106–43 B.C.)

An acquaintance of mine named Lisa Chan possesses a sharp intuition that has tapped into extraordinary streaks of luck. When she lived in Hong Kong during the 1980s, she visited the Happy Valley racetrack and for the first time in her life bet on the horses. She felt no attachment to the outcome of her betting. She simply enjoyed sizing up the horses and their jockeys and giving playful, full rein to her intuition to choose the winners. Nine races were held that day and Lisa picked the winner every time. By the fifth or sixth race, her Chinese friends were placing winning wagers in the thousands of dollars based on her picks, while she continued betting just a few dollars at a time, not taking it seriously. She became a legend in her own time that day at the racetrack.

This practice of duplicating the bets made by a novice woman bettor seems to have a proven track record. Veteran horse race bettor Armando Benitez, in his book *Fate, Coincidence and the Outcome of Horse Races*, claimed his most successful formula for winning at the track always came when he took a woman, preferably a newcomer to race betting, and let her intuitive picks be his guide. This made him a devotee of "beginner's luck," a subject we explore more thoroughly in Part Three.

A few years after her racetrack success, Lisa was living in Los Angeles with her husband, Edward Kovach. One night she had a vivid dream in which she picked the winning numbers in the California lottery. When she awoke she only remembered four of the numbers, so she and Edward played them in the next lottery drawing, supplemented by two others chosen at random. Her dream proved prophetic. Those exact four numbers were picked in the drawing, but not the other two they chose at random, and they collected nearly $1,000 in winnings. Once again, Lisa had demonstrated her gift of periodically becoming an open, intuitive channel.

In researching this book I came across numerous other examples of dreams foretelling the winning numbers in lottery drawings. A retired sheet-metal craftsman, Charlie Kellner, had a series of such "lucky" dreams in the 1970s, which he related to *Time* magazine editor Max Gunther. In the first, Kellner dreamt that he was reading out a house number, #283, and shouting that number up and down the street. After awakening he played that number in the New Jersey "Pick-It" game that day and won. A few days later he dreamt about his deceased mother and her house, so he bet her old house number, #539, and won again. He continued using dream numbers for the rest of the month, and then, as mysteriously as it appeared, his talent for precognition vanished and never returned.

Sometimes these "lucky" dreams project far into the future, accurately sketching a scene years before the actual event. At the age of eighteen, Harry Maertins dreamt that his luck would make him a millionaire by the age of forty, a dream that came to him so vividly he had an unnerving confidence about its resolution for the next twenty-one years of his life. On April 2, 2002, one month before his fortieth birthday, Maertins won one million dollars in the Canadian lottery with a ticket he had purchased at a car wash in Winnipeg, Manitoba.

For every such lottery story of a dream bearing luck and riches that was acted upon and fulfilled, I suspect there are hundreds of other stories about numbers appearing in dreams that were discounted or forgotten. A Boston-area intuitive and author, Lynn Robinson, sent me the following account of her own experience with a lucky dream:

A few months after I was married to my husband, Gary, I woke up early one Wednesday morning with six numbers running through my head. I found I could neither fall back to sleep nor stop the numbers from endlessly repeating themselves in my mind.

I had never played a lottery before, but it occurred to me that these numbers might represent a lottery win. Gary was snoring beside me. I shook him gently and said, "How many numbers are in the Massachusetts state lottery?"

"Six," came his mumbled response.

"I think I might have the winning lottery number," I replied.

He was on his feet, grabbed a paper and pen, and was ready to write down the numbers before I barely had the previous words out of my mouth. I've never seen him wake up that fast since!

With the "winning numbers" in hand, Gary agreed to play them in the Wednesday lottery. I promptly put the whole thing out of my mind until Friday morning when I casually asked if he'd checked on whether our number had won. He confessed that he'd had a crisis at work and had forgotten to play the game on Wednesday.

We took out the newspaper to find the lottery list. You guessed it . . . my numbers were the winning numbers for 15.2 *million dollars* on Wednesday. The same day I received the information and the day he *didn't* play it. So close and yet so far away.

A similar missed opportunity happened to a woman in South Africa, an acquaintance of former *Psychology Today* editor Marc Ian Barasch. She had prayed to receive money to help pay her bills, and in the aftermath had a dream in which her grandfather gave her six numbers to use in obtaining a new house. When Thelma woke up she thought she had been given a phone number, but she also realized it could be numbers for the next South African lottery drawing. She disregarded the dream and failed to buy a lottery ticket. "Then the next day, I saw the winning number was exactly the one in my dream," she confessed to Barasch. "I cried for a week—it paid out a million rand."

What is it about our dream states, I wonder, that sometimes facilitates a percolating of information about the future into our conscious awareness? Can we willfully enhance this precognitive process by programming the content of our dreams? Can we translate the language of dreams and access a hidden wealth of unconscious knowledge to influence, if not predict, our future fortunes?

Seeking Guidance from Dreams

Each of us, if we are average people with average sleep needs, dreams about ninety minutes during every eight-hour period of sleep, which works out to about five years of an average lifetime spent in a dream state. Imagine that. You spend five years of your life having experiences that you mostly forget immediately upon waking. Those of you who remember two or three dreams a week are fortunate. Those of you who remember two or three dreams *a night* are blessed. Those of you who remember that many dreams and translate their meaning and then *act* upon what you have learned, are very lucky indeed.

Why should you care whether you remember any of those often bizarre and apparently meaningless images from sleep? Another book could be written, and many certainly have been, explaining all of the reasons why dreams are important, but allow me to cite just two. Once we utilize a technique to crack the symbolic code of dreams, they can help us to identify and resolve the often repressed issues and conflicts of our emotional lives. The fewer personal issues you have to clutter your consciousness, the more clarity of mind and intuition you have to capitalize on luck opportunities. Second, and most important for the purposes of this book, dreams sometimes channel luck information into our conscious awareness that we would be foolish to ignore.

Dreams occur in patterns, and patterns recur in our dreams. You can't just track the dream images with your rational mind. It must be an intuitive process (there's that word again!). Every dream has a mystery and a force and a feeling at the core of it. Our role is to get involved with the forces at work in our dreams, and be alert to the appearance of information that may provide us with snapshots of possible futures.

When we dream, our brains switch off sensory input from the outside world. Rodolfo Llinas of the New York University School of Medicine suggests that the same process occurs when we are daydreaming, or in a trance, or in hallucinatory states. Some of our clearest dream messages come during the periods of transition from waking to sleep, and from sleep to wakefulness.

Precognitions are foreshadowings of future events—also called premonitions—which cannot be inferred or projected from our current knowledge. Many precognitive dreams will become reality no matter what we do. But others simply present us with possibilities about the future.

Marc Ian Barasch, in his book *Healing Dreams,* writes how "it is fairly certain that if you watch your dreams closely, you will find occasional instances of outright prediction. These are usually odd bits of trivia—you dream about a friend you haven't seen in ten years, and she calls the next day, or an image from a dream shows up in a movie you see a week later." Precognitive dreams "batter down our usual ideas of time in a hailstorm of paradox. They force us to revise our most hallowed axioms about causality itself."

In most precognitive dreams, according to dream researchers, the images feel realistic rather than symbolic, and most, though not all, concern events that will occur over the next twenty-four hours. Because precognitive dreams seem more vivid than ordinary dreams, the details tend to persist in our waking minds long afterward. They leave an echo that Tibetans call "memories of the future."

Precognitive dreaming may have been an adaptive trait that

evolved in our pre-Ice Age ancestors, and which, much like intuition, conferred certain evolutionary advantages. Everyday life among hunter-gatherers must have been a life-or-death gamble, with survival in every waking or sleeping hour dependent on anticipating the most unpredictable encounter with a saber-toothed tiger or a human predator. Precognition reduced the margins of chance, and those who used it most effectively were the luckiest.

Throughout both the Old and New Testaments of the Bible can be found descriptions of precognitive dreams and intuitive predictions. In the Old Testament, as you may recall, Joseph correctly interpreted the Pharaoh of Egypt's dream about seven lean cows being eaten by seven fat cows to mean that seven years of good harvest would be followed by seven years of famine. In the New Testament, a day after the birth of Jesus, his father Joseph received a warning in a dream to flee with Mary and Jesus to Egypt, an act saving Jesus from King Herod's slaughter of firstborn male children.

Precognitive dreams are apparently more common than we would suspect. In 1974, an extensive psi survey of residents and students in Charlottesville, Virginia, by two researchers showed how widespread this form of dreaming may be. More than 350 town residents and 262 students at the University of Virginia answered forty-six questions about psi experiences, including this one: "Have you ever had a rather clear and specific dream which matched in detail an event which occurred before, during, or after your dream, and which you did not know about or did not expect at the time of the dream?" Answers in the affirmative were given by thirty-eight percent of students and thirty-six percent of town residents. These same people were also more likely than other survey respondents to have experienced other types of psi events.

Under the category of guidance dreams, those that are precognitive stand out. "Often the imagery is startlingly vivid," observes Judith Orloff, the psychiatrist who documented her own precognitions in *Second Sight*. "You may be given information clarifying times, dates, places, or the direction your life is going to take. . . . Precognitive dreams can be a precursor of blessings to come, or often underlying meaning about more difficult times."

Some of the more persuasive experimental evidence demonstrating that we experience precognition and other psi effects in our dreams comes from studies in the 1960s and 1970s at the Dream Laboratory hosted by the Maimonides Medical Center in New York City. Its primary researcher for many years was Montague Ullman, a professor emeritus of clinical psychiatry at the Albert Einstein College of Medicine. Dr. Ullman consistently found that our unconscious dreaming selves exhibit a wisdom beyond what we know in our conscious waking states. His most successful dream studies, in which someone awake tried to send an image mentally to someone dreaming, occurred when the images were emotionally compelling to the dreamer.

These sorts of cases seem to indicate that our brain's state during dreaming makes it more open to channeling information beyond our ordinary sensory awareness. "It seems more than coincidence that such psychic experiences should occur during the period when normal sensory input to the brain is sharply curtailed," says Dr. Richard Broughton, author of *Parapsychology: The Controversial Science*. "This is the time when the brain is not busy processing the welter of sensory information, nor is it busy manipulating memory images for future activities. Is there something about the brain's activity during REM (rapid eye movement) that facilitates the expression of ESP?"

Precognitive Dreams of Misfortune

Within my own family, stories of good luck, bad luck streaks, and premonitions are a growing collection of mysteries that we marvel at with each retelling. My mother's one and only precognitive dream, at least that she can recall, ranks near the top of my list of dreams that exemplify our capacity to experience premonitions of peril.

When she was twenty-five years old and six months pregnant with me, my mother dreamt that one of my father's co-workers on an oil rig rang the doorbell downstairs, and the landlady, a Mrs.

Martin, was awakened and answered the door. The oil field worker informed her that my father had been seriously injured in a drilling rig accident and had been taken to a hospital. In the dream Mrs. Martin came up the stairs, knocked on my mother's door, and relayed this distressing news. At that point the dream ended. My mother woke up and lay in bed for several hours in a disturbed state, thinking about this dream.

She had the dream about midnight. At around this same time, my father was working the night shift at an oil rig twenty miles outside San Angelo, in West Texas, when a thirty-foot length of drilling pipe fell inside the derrick and struck him in the head and back. He was paralyzed from the waist down, and suffered a concussion and a broken foot and ankle.

As my mother lay awake in the aftermath of the dream, she heard the doorbell ring downstairs at 2:30 A.M. The dream had felt so real to her that as the events unfolded, exactly mirroring the details of her dream, she remained calm, feeling as if she were watching a scene from a movie about her life. Mrs. Martin walked up the stairs and knocked. My mother opened the door, knowing just what the landlady would say.

"Truman's been hurt at the job," said Mrs. Martin. "They want you at the hospital."

Mrs. Martin held a box of tissues, but she was more upset than my mother, who kept thinking to herself, "I've already been through this. It has already happened."

The dream had prepared my mother emotionally for the jolting news, and helped her to summon the strength she needed over the next few months as my father recovered in the hospital. She recorded this dream, as she has all of the daily events in her life, in a series of diaries that she has kept for more than fifty years. My father eventually recovered from the paralysis, prompting the doctors to call him a very lucky man. Read more about his many brushes with death in Part Three.

Dreams of bad luck often involve people we don't know and events not directly connected to us. For ten consecutive nights during May 1979, David Booth had a recurring nightmare that never varied in its details. The 27-year-old Booth, a Cincinnati car rental agency manager, described his dream to magazine writer Walter Lowe: "I'm looking out over a field and there's, like, a line of trees going down and I look up in the air and there's an American Airlines jet, a great big thing, and the first thing that strikes me is it just isn't making the noise it should for being that close.

"Then it starts to bank off and the left wing goes up in the air and it's going very slow, and then it just turned on its back and went straight down into the ground and exploded." As the crash thundered in his dreaming mind, Booth woke up, night after night, always in tears.

"Although I'm calling this thing a dream," Booth continued, "it wasn't like a dream at all. Only someone who has had this happen to him will know what I mean when I say that it was real. I remember it like you remember a real experience, not like you remember a dream. That's the difference."

Feeling certain his dream was reflecting a future reality, Booth called the Federal Aviation Administration and related the dream to Ray Pinkerton, the assistant manager for Cincinnati airway facilities. Pinkerton was impressed by Booth's sincerity and took notes on their conversation. Afterwards, Pinkerton called the FAA regional office in Atlanta and described the dream to public affairs officer Jack Barker. But there was nothing Barker felt he could do, if only because the dream didn't contain a date or time or other identifying features.

The afternoon after Booth's tenth and final repeat of the dream, American Airlines flight 191 left Chicago's O'Hare Airport for Los Angeles. During takeoff the plane lost an engine and rolled to the left, slammed into the ground and exploded, killing all 271 people on board. "No one," wrote Lowe in a 1980 *Playboy* article, "not even the FAA, questions the uncanny similarity between major details of Booth's vision and the actual crash."

When reporters asked a vice president for American Airlines what would be done in the future if he received a dream report like Booth's describing an accident, the executive scoffed at the suggestion that it should ever be taken seriously. "I'd ignore it. We discount the occult here. It goes against everything scientific and logical to even discuss such a damn thing as a dream."

We really can't fault the airline executive for his attitude. Undoubtedly, American and the other airlines receive scores of accident warnings every year that never come true. Prudent executives simply can't afford to heed everyone who wakes up certain he or she has glimpsed a future tragedy. And yet . . . there is a twist to this particular story.

A few months before the flight 191 crash, 34-year-old ex-model Shawn Robbins, a gifted New York intuitive whom I had interviewed for an unrelated article in 1980, appeared on a series of radio shows with her own warning of disaster. She predicted, based on a premonition, that an American Airlines plane flying to the West Coast out of Chicago's O'Hare Airport would crash due to a mechanical problem. She made this prediction on radio talk shows in Cincinnati, Savannah, and Tulsa. (Whether Booth heard her on the Cincinnati station, we don't know, but the possible connection is curious.)

How often do multiple dreamers, like Booth and Robbins, have the same or similar premonitions about future events? Can we possibly separate false prophets from persons channeling accurate information based on the early warning systems of intuition filtering through their dream states?

At the macro level of large-scale disasters, human skepticism will probably always create barriers to any institutional acceptance of precognitive information, no matter how reliable the individual source or sources prove themselves. It may be that certain intuited macro events on the world stage are unavoidable, destined to happen even with sufficient warning. Of the nineteen most well-documented cases of precognition foretelling the sinking of the *Titanic*, nearly all came from dreams, and while many of the dreamers chose not to board the ship as a result, their fears never came close to reaching the critical threshold of influencing the mass consciousness of other passengers, or even the mindsets of the *Titanic*'s owners and crew. Under probability theory, chance is expected to exact a minimum number of casualties over time to satisfy the law of averages.

Dreams Foretelling September 11

The horrific carnage of September 11, 2001, provides another window into the interrelationship of mass consciousness, precognitive dreams, and global events. Not until just before the nineteen hijackers boarded the four ill-fated airline flights on that day did most of them learn they were on a suicide mission. That was one of the revelations from a video of boastful statements made by Osama bin Laden, reportedly taped in Afghanistan on November 5, 2001, during the American bombing campaign, and released worldwide on December 13 by the Pentagon.

Half of the videotape, the half that few people remember because the media generally ignored it, featured Bin Laden discussing the concerns he had felt before the attack that precognitive dreams his followers were having, dreams about planes crashing into American buildings, might compromise the secrecy of his plans. Numerous members of Bin Laden's terror support network who were not aware of details concerning the plot apparently dreamt the general themes and even specific aspects of what would occur.

According to Bin Laden's account on the tape, a man named Abu al-Hasan, who was not a part of the plot, had related the following dream to him a year earlier, when the hijacking was still in the planning stages. "I saw in a dream we were playing a soccer game against the Americans. When our team showed up on the field, they were all pilots! So I wondered if that was a soccer game or a pilot game? Our players were pilots. And we defeated them."

A religious official sitting with Bin Laden during the taping describes a dream that had been related by one of his associates. In it were "people who left for jihad and they found themselves in Washington and New York. I have another man . . . my God . . . he said and swore by Allah that his wife had seen the incident a week earlier. She had seen the plane crashing into a building."

It is at this point on the videotape that Bin Laden made his revelation about the hijackers not knowing their mission in advance. "We did not reveal the operation to them until they were there and just before they boarded the planes." Then Bin Laden described a dream by still another follower that involved tall buildings in America.

"At that point," concedes Bin Laden, "I was worried that maybe the secret would be revealed if everyone starts seeing it in their dream."

In the aftermath of 9/11, hundreds of reports surfaced worldwide from people who believed they had dreamt the tragedy in advance. Some of these dreams were posted on Web sites, or shared with dream study groups before the tragedy unfolded, so there is no hint of deception or exaggeration. For example, a woman in Los Angeles named Katy shared a dream by e-mail with her dream circle on August 30, in which she saw four planes crashing on a single day.

Among my own circle of friends, many of whom keep dream journals, and all of them eminently trustable, several recorded dreams that seemed to anticipate 9/11. Liza Leeds is a movie producer and a jewelry designer whom I have sat with in dreamworking circles over the years. Liza is the sort of natural intuitive who thinks of someone and within minutes that person will call. She had this dream on the night of September, 6, 2001.

"I dreamt I was sitting in my car in Manhattan. It was unnaturally quiet. A policeman taps on my window and tells me to move my car. I know something is terribly wrong. I look uptown and it's completely dark and debris is everywhere. Cars are flattened. It looks like a war zone. Out of the debris four firemen walk toward my car. They tell me that a building has exploded. When I woke up, the dream had so upset me, it felt like such a big dream, that I immediately wrote it down. I just knew at the time that it was a precognitive dream."

Precognition and Personal Luck

At the personal level, in the micro realm of our daily existence, our luck can change in accordance with our attention to precognitive information, whether it originates in our intuitive waking or dreaming states. Just before his assassination, Roman Emperor Julius Caesar ignored the warnings of his wife, Calpurnia, who had two dreams in a single night—one literal, the other symbolic—portraying her husband's murder. Imagine that Caesar had heeded her fears, rather than brushed them off as superstition, and had been alerted to uncover the plot against him. He might have gotten lucky and lived longer, and accomplished more, though the most significant events of history might otherwise have remained largely unaltered.

Days before his own death at the hands of assassin John Wilkes Booth, President Abraham Lincoln dreamed vividly of the aftermath of his assassination, and confided the details to his friend Ward Lamon, the U.S. Marshal for the District of Columbia. Lamon documented the dream in his diary, providing the narrative just as Lincoln had related it.

"About ten days ago, I retired very late. . . . I soon began to dream. There seemed to be a deathlike stillness about me. Then I heard subdued sobs, as if a number of people were weeping. I thought I left my bed and wandered downstairs. . . . I went from room to room. No living person was in sight, but the same mournful sounds of distress met me as I passed along. It was light in all the rooms, but where were all the people who were grieving as if their hearts would break? I was puzzled and alarmed. Determined to find the cause of a state of affairs so mysterious, and so shocking, I kept on until I arrived in the East Room, which I entered. There I met with a sickening surprise. Before me was a catafalque, on which rested a corpse in funeral vestments. Around it were stationed soldiers who were acting as guards, and there was a throng of people, some gazing mournfully upon the corpse, whose face was covered. . . .

"Who is dead in the White House?" I demanded of one of the soldiers.

"The President," was his answer. "He was killed by an assassin."

Those among us prone to speculations about such matters can't help but wonder what would have happened if Marshal Lamon, or Lincoln himself, had taken this dream seriously enough to, at the very least, double the guard around the President. The assassin was only able to barge into the theater booth and shoot Lincoln because the single guard on duty had taken a break and left his post. A lucky break for the assassin became a huge misfortune for the nation struggling to heal the wounds of Civil War.

A 1961 book by Arthur Osborn, *The Future Is Now*, describes the results of an intriguing precognition experiment in which the French actress Irene Muza was placed in a dreamlike state through hypnosis and asked to "see" and describe her future. She cryptically responded with, "My career will be short. I dare not say what my end will be. It will be terrible."

Before being brought out of her trance, the precognition researchers gave Muza a posthypnotic suggestion that she would not remember anything she had said. Nor did these researchers afterwards tell her what had been related. In his book, *The Holographic Universe,* Michael Talbot finishes her story. "Even if she had known, it would not have caused the type of death she suffered. A few months later her hairdresser accidentally spilled some mineral spirits on a lighted stove, causing Muza's hair and clothing to be set on fire. Within seconds she was engulfed in flames and died in a hospital a few hours later."

An obvious question emerges from the experiences of people who have glimpsed tragic events. Could they have avoided the bad luck that befell them or helped to avoid it for others? "Put another way," writes Michael Talbot, "is the future frozen and completely predetermined, or can it be changed? At first blush, the existence of precognitive phenomena seems to indicate that the former is the case, but this would be a very disturbing state of affairs. If the future is a hologram whose every detail is already fixed, it means that we have no free will. We are all just puppets of destiny moving mindlessly through a script that has already been written. Fortunately, the evidence overwhelmingly indicates that this is not the case. The literature is filled with examples of people who were able to use their precognitive glimpses of the future to avoid disasters."

One of the twentieth century's most creative physicists, David Bohm, believed that the universe, the human brain, and the future are all holographic in principle. "When people dream of accidents correctly and do not take the plane or ship," Bohm wrote, "it is not the actual future that they were seeing. It was merely something in the present which is implicate and moving toward making that future. In fact, the future they saw differed from the actual future because they altered it. . . . As they used to say, coming events cast their shadows in the present."

As Talbot and others point out, not all dreams of accidents, death, and disaster are disregarded, or not acted upon. One such dream may have saved the life of psychologist Marcia Emery. As she relates in her book *PowerHunch!*, "In the dream, I was driving a car, put my foot on the brake, and it went right to the floor." A week later Emery was driving along a street in Washington, D.C., when the brakes on her car failed. Her foot went right to the floorboard, just as it had in the dream, and the emergency brake also failed. "My dream had alerted me to this possibility, and my intuitive voice told me to make a quick right. I did, and the car came to a stop." Needless to say, Dr. Emery considered herself both blessed and lucky.

Precognitive Dreams of Fortune

Among gamblers the precognitive dream that foretells their big win is the one dream of their life they will probably never forget. During my interviews with slot and video poker players who regularly won at the Konocti Vista Casino, three players volunteered the details of recent precognitive dreams that had yielded monetary rewards.

Lonna Young is a rental property owner whose initials LKY symbolize to her the feeling of being a lucky person. She had taken up playing slot machines and Joker Poker after her partner of fourteen years died of cancer. Just a few weeks before I interviewed Lonna, an unforgettable dream had visited her. "It was a very vivid dream and I ordinarily don't ever remember my dreams when I wake up. I dreamt that I got five jacks on video poker. I could see the particular machine to play. A day later I went to Konocti. I sat down at a video poker machine just like the one in my dream, and I quickly won one thousand dollars with five jacks. I was shocked. Quite pleasantly so."

Luck embraced real estate agent Dorothy Walker in a similar fashion. At the time she had her precognitive dream, she was alternating her dollar and half-dollar slot playing time between Konocti and several casinos in Reno, Nevada. "I had this dream about one particular machine in one particular casino in Reno," Dorothy told me. "I could visualize where the machine was located in the casino. In the dream I played it and won big, but I didn't know how much because I woke up at that moment. About a month passed before my husband and I went to Reno again. I went looking for that machine and found it. I put in one hundred dollars and within a few minutes hit a five thousand dollar jackpot. I was so happy that I had followed the dream. I'm always sorry afterwards if I don't follow my hunches."

My first encounter with Vince Syphax came on his seventy-eighth birthday. He and his wife, Josephine, were celebrating by playing the quarter and dollar slots at Konocti. I happened to be standing next to Josephine when she dropped three dollars into a machine and immediately hit three of the doubler symbols on the payline for a $2,400 jackpot. A few minutes later, Vince sat down next to me at a quarter machine and started hitting a series of small jackpots. I struck up a conversation with him, and this retired dispatcher for Southern Pacific Railroad told me about the dream he had had a few weeks earlier.

"I was at home in Lakeport playing a computer program of slots, the red, white, and blue version of the machine. I kept getting three white sevens repeatedly on this program and I had never hit that combination before. That night I had a dream that I was playing on a particular machine and hit three white sevens. So the next morning I went to Robinson Rancheria Casino (another Pomo Indian casino on the other side of Clear Lake from Konocti). And everything happened just exactly as it did in the dream. I found the machine I had seen in the dream, a quarter machine. I sat down and almost immediately hit three white sevens for three hundred dollars. I was so excited. I was telling everybody, 'I had a dream of hitting this last night!' "

Dreams of Horse Race Winners

The more widely that I cast my research net, the more striking the variety and numbers of lucky dream stories that turned up. A Jungian psychologist in England named Stan Gooch, an acquaintance of mine from a trip I made to London in 1979, has collected a vast array of his own precognitive dreams that yielded monetary rewards in an unusual way—betting on horses at the racetrack.

In the first of these dreams, Gooch was at the cinema with friends and felt a tremendous enthusiasm for the movie, though Gooch could remember nothing about the film except its name, *Showman's Fair*. The next morning after the dream, Gooch happened to read in the newspaper that a horse named Showman's Fair was running in a race that day. Ordinarily this would never have been a horse Gooch would bet on, since at eleven years of age the animal was long past normal retirement. Gooch followed his intuition about the dream and bet $10 on the horse. It won the race at a 7 to 2 payout. A week later the horse ran again and won, earning Gooch more money. Then the horse was permanently retired from racing.

In the United States, a medical psychologist and professor at the University of California at Los Angeles, Dr. Thelma Moss, director of the Neuropsychiatric Institute, undertook a study of precognitive dreams during the 1970s and found numerous persons who periodically dreamt about the winners of horse races. One of these lucky dreamers was Dr. Moss's personal friend, Mrs. Sammie Hudson, a school psychologist.

Mrs. Hudson had no interest in racing or gambling, and she rarely remembered her dreams, yet she began having vivid dreams about horse races—dreams she remembered on waking—two or three times a week over a period of four months. In each of these colorful dreams, she heard the race announcer clearly state the

winning horses' names in a strong, clear voice. She told her husband and he began finding those names among the lists of horses
racing each week in various parts of the nation. He bet on each of
those horses and he consistently won.

"Eventually they won enough money to buy a luxury automobile," reported Dr. Moss in her book, *The Probability of the Impossible*. "Immediately after they bought the car, her dreams of horse
races stopped." Several years later, however, Mrs. Hudson had a
persistent and clear dream about winning a Las Vegas casino jackpot. She and her husband drove to Las Vegas and, yes, she won a
sizable jackpot, but afterwards those dreams, too, disappeared from
her conscious awareness.

A second horse race dreamer, also described by Dr. Moss in her
book, was a bookkeeper, a devout Catholic, who had resisted betting on the horses that appeared in her dreams out of a religious
objection to gambling. For years she had remembered dreams in
which she would see a winning horse cross the finish line, and she
would clearly see the winning horse's number. Her husband, an insurance broker, wanted to test her dreams by betting on her picks
at the racetrack. One morning, apparently to appease him, "she announced that if they went to the track that day and played the daily
double, they might win a thousand dollars. She had seen two races
being run in a single dream, and she remembered not only the
horses' numbers but the odds on the daily double. They went to
the track and for their two dollars they received nearly one thousand dollars, just as she had dreamed."

One of the more remarkable accounts of a racetrack dream that
came true was provided to Dr. Moss by a television producer in Los
Angeles. The only precognitive dream of his life involved a horse
race, despite the fact that horse racing had never interested him. In
the dream two horses were in a photo finish, as described by an excited TV announcer who broadcast the name of the winner. When
the producer awoke he remembered the horse's name and realized
that he had a friend who had once owned a horse by that name.
The horse had been sold. On a hunch, the producer searched a

newspaper for races occurring the next day and found the horse's name. Dr. Moss picks up his story. "Fortunately for psychic research, the next morning he told his office staff about the dream, and they all decided to take pieces of a large bet on the horse to win. The TV producer reported that watching the race on television was one of the uncanny experiences of his life because he had already seen it in his dream. As in the dream, the announcer's voice mounted with excitement as the race drew to a photo finish, and his horse was the winner."

From the preceding three stories, Dr. Moss uncovered a pattern that revealed valuable information about how our personalities and professional training tend to shape the contents of precognitive messages. In the case of Mrs. Hudson, the psychologist, she heard the names of winners, just as in her professional life she heard the stories of her clients. In the example of the bookkeeper, she saw the winning numbers of horses crossing the finish line, just as in her professional life she dealt every day with numbers. As for the TV producer, he saw the race as a televised event, much as he envisioned scenes for broadcast in his professional life.

"These details," concluded Dr. Moss, "lend credence to the theory that biocommunication arrives at an unconscious level, and must rise up through the personal unconscious, receiving on the way to the surface the distortions of primary process, molded by the personality of the receiver."

Needless to say, it is not only in the realm of gambling that we find "lucky" dreams and dreamers. Scientists have sometimes dreamt their greatest scientific discoveries. Niels Bohr, the Nobel Prize-winning physicist, confessed that he dreamt his model of the atom. Otto Loewi admitted that he dreamt his experiment with frogs' nerves that led to his eventual Nobel Prize.

After studying a wide range of dream reports and experiments in precognition from ninety years of collected data, Dr. Robert L. Van de Castle, a professor of clinical psychology at the University of Virginia Medical Center, found "very encouraging evidence" that precognition had been "demonstrated under good experimental conditions." He reached some tentative conclusions about these lucky dreamers:

- nearly twice as many women as men have, or at least report, paranormal dreams.
- death is a theme in these types of dreams half of the time, with accidents next in order of occurrence.
- these dreams, in contrast to "normal" dreaming, are "unusually vivid and intense," and "have a peculiarly tenacious quality to them after a dreamer awakens."

A series of dream and psi studies from Sweden and Iceland in 1968 and 1975 revealed the following: people who recalled one or more dreams each week scored considerably higher on clairvoyance and precognition tests than did persons who don't normally remember their dreams; and, people with frequent dream recall also report more precognitive dreams.

"Not only are dreams relatively frequent carriers of paranormal information," remarked Stan Gooch, "but for a great many individuals, their one and only paranormal experience occurs in a dream. We could say that in a sense it is the ability to carry the dream state into waking life which constitutes being psychic."

Commodities Market Dreamers

Missouri commodities broker J. P. Dixon vividly remembered a dream he had one night in 1975, when he was thirty-five years old, that featured a coffee crop still on the bush in Colombia, accompanied by the image of a ticker tape emblazoned with the figure of 4200 British pounds Sterling. He interpreted this figure to be the coffee price per pound. For weeks afterward Dixon puzzled over the dream, wondering whether, like most dreams, it only had symbolic meaning. He knew the price of coffee in British pounds had never gone over 500 Sterling before. Yet, for some reason he felt an unwavering faith in the accuracy of the dream.

"I felt the dream was true to the marrow of my bones," Dixon, now retired in Texas, told me. "Previously in my life I had the experience of picking exact scores in basketball games or hearing an intuitive voice telling me to buy silver or to purchase real estate. But this was different. I didn't tell people about the dream because they might have thought I was a wacko."

A synchronicity intervened to confirm for Dixon that the dream demanded he take action. He happened to see Beverly Jaegers, who lived in the St. Louis area, interviewed on a television program about her work as a "psychic detective," providing her "remote viewing" skills as a public service to police departments trying to solve difficult criminal cases. In her mind's eye, Jaegers would try to visualize the location of missing people, or important pieces of evidence connected to crimes. As Dixon listened to Jaegers, he got an intuitive hit that maybe her gift could be applied to his own line of work. "After seeing Beverly on television I had an overwhelming compulsion to talk with her. It was like a mission and I couldn't put my finger on why."

He phoned her and inquired whether her remote viewing technique would work as well in business as it seemed to in crime. Not knowing the answer, Jaegers suggested they try an experiment. She asked him to write his question down on a piece of paper and seal it in an envelope, then come to her office the next Saturday so she could attempt to remotely view the question and answer. Dixon arrived as planned and handed her the envelope. She also asked for his keys. She held the ring of keys in her left hand, feeling into what they helped tell her about Dixon.

"What is Harlingen?" she suddenly asked.

"That's the town in southern Texas where I was born," Dixon replied, trying not to show his surprise.

"What is Deaf Smith to you?"

"That's the county in Texas where I grew up."

This exchange went on for a few minutes, Beverly Jaegers continuing to sketch J. P. Dixon's life using details no stranger should have known about him. *This is really neat*, Dixon thought; *no wonder she can catch criminals.*

After "reading" him and relaying her impressions, she took the sealed envelope in her left hand and began to feel into what she "saw" in her mind's eye. "This is strange," she commented, and proceeded to describe for Dixon the image she had of bushes with small, cherrylike fruit that had become shriveled, as if dying from harsh weather.

A wide smile spread across Dixon's face as he opened the envelope and showed Jaegers a brochure about coffee futures, featuring a photo of a coffee bush with its distinctive berries. He told her about the dream he had of the coffee crop and the number that had appeared, presumably a price. Her reading had added the element of the crop's failure due to bad weather. So he asked the obvious question: "When do you see this happening?" Jaegers didn't know, but she felt certain his dream and the image she had remotely viewed were precognitive glimpses of a future reality.

Convinced now that he was clued in to something important, Dixon pulled $24,000 out of his bank account and invested it all on coffee futures contracts at $200 per contract. He drew up a sign saying "COFFEE @ 2,900" (2900 was the figure Jaegers had seen in her vision) and attached it to the wall near his office desk. At Dixon's urging, his friend Logan Mock, and Logan's mother, Jane Mock, also invested heavily in coffee futures.

"I wasn't skeptical," Logan Mock explained in an interview with me years later. "My mother had a reading from Beverly and was impressed with her. And I've had feelings about how things would happen since I was a child. I felt like these coffee options could be a big thing. Timing is the problem. That's where your own intuition comes in. There may also be signs along the way. Beverly had that one nailed. It fell into place beautifully."

Several months after Jaegers seemed to confirm Dixon's dream, a severe freeze ruined the Colombian coffee crop and prices more than doubled, creating an incentive for Dixon to sell, as most commodity futures traders would have done after just a few weeks. Yet, Dixon overcame his nervousness, kept his contracts, and even bought more, anticipating that the price he had seen in the dream would eventually materialize.

Dixon paid another visit to Jaegers with a new sealed envelope in hand. As she did her reading she was puzzled to visualize Russian tanks rolling over fields of bushes, followed by scenes of businessmen fleeing and soldiers burning sacks of something stored in warehouses. Inside the envelope, Dixon had placed a newspaper clipping about the prospect of a Russian-backed military threat to Angola, the world's second-largest coffee producer. Several weeks after Jaeger's reading for Dixon, the civil war in Angola began, sending the London market price for coffee up still higher.

By the spring of 1976, the combination of weather troubles in Colombia and war in Angola had created a severe worldwide shortage of coffee, especially instant coffee, and Dixon's coffee futures, bought at $200 per contract, were now worth more than $9,000 apiece. The number that Dixon had seen in his dream, 4200 British pounds, which might have seemed absurd to most people the previous year, had now been exceeded! J. P. Dixon became a rich man, and his investors, especially Logan Mock and his mother, made small fortunes as well. In appreciation of the help Jaegers had given, Dixon bought Jaegers and her husband, Ray, a ranch-style house, a single-floor model so that Beverly, who suffered from polio, wouldn't have to be burdened with stairs.

Dixon purchased a piece of property he had always coveted and retired to Texas. The precognitive dreams retired with him. "I stopped having the dreams. I don't know why. But I kept playing with the commodities market, and I just started guessing. I made mistakes and that hurt me financially. As I look back I think of what happened to me as blessings rather than luck. Now I speak blessings to everyone I meet."

Beverly Jaegers expanded her exploration of time and its effects on the mind and precognitive viewing. She wanted clearer answers to the question of "when" an event she visualized would occur. Choosing a stockbroker to work with, she began picking stock names at random from a list provided by the brokerage house, placed the names in envelopes, and then tried to visualize a graph of how the stock would perform over the next few months. Though I haven't seen a list of her failures, her successes at using this method were impressive. She bought G. D. Searle Pharmaceutical Company stock at $11 a share and within three months it reached $33 a share. A futures contract she bought in rubber tripled in value within two months. In 1981, the *St. Louis Business Journal* conducted a contest pitting Jaegers against eighteen professional stockbrokers, each picking five stocks they thought would increase in value over a period of months. Her picks beat seventeen of the eighteen stockbrokers. Jaegers died in 2001, a few years after publishing a book, *The Psychic Paradigm,* in which she revealed to readers "the secrets of unlocking your own ESP abilities."

Stock Market Dreamers

A pair of seemingly unrelated dreams on the same night in September 1987, each containing a warning, transformed Walter Stover's entire perspective on the usefulness of his dream life. At the time, he was a resident of Atlanta, Georgia, employed as a chemical research engineer for a major corporation, and making investments in the stock market on the side. He had been periodically working with his dreams for nearly a decade, using dream analysis techniques derived from Edgar Cayce readings, but he had never before experienced and worked with dreams quite like these.

In the first dream, he was on a bus with a group of football players, one of whom warned him not to sit next to the coach because "he knows all the big gains are over." That dream by itself wouldn't have clued Stover to anything, but the second dream got more specific. In it Stover was riding on a train into Washington, D.C., with his financial planner, a man named John. During the ride the two men went into the dining car and loaded up on junk food. In reality both men were health conscious and would never have consumed junk food. When the train entered the Washington, D.C., station everyone got off, yet when Stover and his financial planner tried to board again the conductor adamantly gave excuses why they couldn't get back on the train.

The next morning, after reducing the two dreams into one-sentence themes and combining them based on the Cayce-inspired formula, Stover got, in his words, "a loud, screaming message that I needed to get out of the stock market." He immediately phoned his financial adviser, John, and ordered him to sell the five stocks he was most heavily invested in. For weeks afterward, Stover second-guessed himself with doubts, wondering, "Why have I done this crazy thing?"

A month later the bottom fell out of the stock market with a meltdown of more than 500 points in a single day. Stover saved himself a considerable amount of money by having acted on his intuition about the pair of dreams. "That experience," Stover explained in a conversation he had with me, "proved that I could put my dreams to use in my investing practice."

Since then Stover's financial success at using his dreams to play the stock market has been nothing short of extraordinary. He experiences investment dreams at least five or six times a month, mostly spontaneously, though he does periodically "program" or "incubate" his dreams by thinking of certain stocks as he drifts off to sleep. Some of these precognitive dreams contain quite specific information, such as company names, company logos, or ticker symbols. Most of the investment dream imagery, however, much as with all categories of dreams, appears highly symbolic, and Stover must decipher the meaning based on symbols that appear which are peculiar to him and his own dream history.

One repeating symbolic image is finding money lying on the ground, which tells him whatever subject the dream concerns is what he should buy. That is how he made a killing off a stock called Movie Gallery. He dreamt that he found lots of money in front of a deserted movie theater. At the time Stover bought it, Movie Gallery stock stood at $1.75 per share. He held on to it for over a year until July 2001, when he sold it at $13 per share.

Other symbols appearing in his dreams are universal, such as the bears and bulls that indicate market trends down (bears) and up (bulls). Market expressions and terminology also surface. On September 21, 2001, for instance, deep into the bear market decline of the Dow Jones stock average, Stover dreamt that he saw a man fishing along a river that descended into a canyon seemingly without a bottom. Someone along the canyon's rim threw in a fishing line and announced that it was time to go bottom fishing. That expression, "bottom fishing," is investor slang for buying stocks at the bottom of a market decline. The dream proved prophetic because the market hit its low that day at 8,062, and rallied up to the 10,663 level by March 2002, before undergoing another decline.

As a general rule, Stover finds lag times of two weeks to two years before his precognitive stock dreams come true. He uses technical charts, graphs of daily stock price highs and lows, to supplement his intuition on decisions about when to buy or sell the stocks selected by his dreams.

To satisfy his curiosity about other people's precognitive investment dreams, Stover did a search in 1998 via the Internet and through Edgar Cayce-related outlets. A dream group gradually formed in which about two dozen people scattered across the United States, Canada, and Australia, share their precognitive stock investment dreams on-line, producing an average of about twenty per month (their Web site is: www.webspawner.com/users/stockdreams/index.html.)

Several members of the group are not strictly dreamers—they tend to receive direct intuitive information on stocks. Membership requirements for the group are exacting: a person needs to have been an active investor for five years, and must have had ten precognitive dreams in the previous three years. Stover also places a warning label on membership: "Investing via dream information needs to be approached with some caution. My own dreams are *not* 100 percent accurate and reliable. About two-thirds produce strong, positive results over a period of several years. The other one-third produce losses. This means that one needs to invest in a group of these stocks and not attempt to make a quick killing in just one or two."

A "Paranormal" Betting System

Through Walt Stover and his dream group, I located and interviewed a retired computer marketing executive in Texas and a practicing psychologist in New York who have integrated into daily life their respective processes of precognitive dream "incubation," resulting in significant enhancements to their financial prosperity. The first man asked that I not use his real name. He feared that doing so might alert Las Vegas bookmakers to his use of a paranormal betting system and result in their refusal to take his bets. So I will refer to him as Mr. Boyd.

Mr. Boyd first recognized his precognitive dream ability in 1993 when he dreamt about one specific play in a forthcoming college football game between Syracuse and his alma mater, the University of Texas at Austin. In the dream a Texas kicker punted the football and it traveled down the left side of the field, a long punt of sixty-five yards, heading toward the south end zone and then bouncing into it for a touchback. During the actual game, as Boyd watched on television, this same play with these very details unfolded. The game was otherwise boring and ended in a tie, but this particular play haunted Boyd for weeks afterward. He couldn't get the prophetic dream image out of his mind.

"Never again would I have the same view of reality. I kept asking myself, what was this precognitive dream trying to tell me? I believed that I had a message from God and I'd better try to figure it out. Intuitively, I was certain of this. It was the overriding thought in my mind for a long time."

A few months later Boyd took a non-credit course on dreams under the auspices of the student union at the University of Texas. He found the sessions instructive, but the most important material it produced for him was a bibliography of books on dreams, and in that list he discovered several books that described methods and exercises for "incubating" or "programming" the subject matter of dreams. Boyd combined some of these techniques with a self-hypnosis tape he created so he could have "lucid" dreams—the act of dreaming while you are aware that you are dreaming.

Over the next decade he systematically—and, quite often, successfully—applied this dream approach to betting on sports events. Here is an example of how he incubated and then worked a dream sequence. On September 6, 1999, he played his relaxation tape and programmed his dreams to pick a group of winners that were underdogs in that weekend's professional football games. In the resulting lucid dream he saw a team in blue jerseys running over an opposing team at will. A second dream followed in which Boyd encountered a friend who needed "one key." Those two dreams together told Boyd that the key to winning would be to bet on a group of three or four teams with jerseys similar to the color of blue in his first dream. He found the three teams that were point-spread underdogs, one being the Dallas Cowboys, and bet $10 on the moneyline of each team. "I'm a conservative bettor," Boyd confessed. All three underdogs triumphed, earning Boyd $700 in winnings.

"I had always thought you had to be a shrink or a psychic to interpret your dreams, but I learned that anyone can be trained to do it," Boyd marveled in a conversation with me. "Beyond just the money I've won, which has been up to $2,000 at a time, working with dreams has shown me so much about myself."

Dr. Arthur Bernard holds the unique distinction of being a psychologist specializing in dream analysis who, in his own dream life, experienced precognitive stock dreams that produced a fortune for him. In 1995, while director of The Dream Center in Sherman Oaks, California, Dr. Bernard received a call from a man who had participated in one of his dream seminars. The man described having had a dream about Bernard and a Biotech stock, ICOS, in which he saw the stock rising from $4 to $10 a share.

Soon thereafter, Dr. Bernard began having his own dreams about ICOS stock. These dreams persisted over the next three years. Despite never having experienced a stock dream prior to these, Dr. Bernard trusted his dream process, and he had also seen precognitive dreams come up frequently among his clients during nearly thirty years of practice as a psychologist. So he began buying shares of the stock, ultimately about 40,000 shares, at prices ranging from $4 to $4.50 per share. This stock became a gold mine for him. When he sold most of it in 1998, it had reached $28 a share, and he pocketed more than $1 million.

"Precognitive dreams are common in my seminars," Dr. Bernard told me in an interview. "Up to thirty percent of the people in my seminars, who are mostly social workers and psychologists, admit to having had them. In my experience, the less conflicted a person is and the less personal material they have to deal with in their dreams, the more likely they are to have precognitive dreams."

Meditation, Hypnosis, and Psi Receptivity

"It seems paradoxical, but more of your brain is awake when you're asleep than when you are in a conscious state," writes neuroscientist Mona Lisa Schulz. "When you're awake, only about ten percent of your brain is firing at any given time. But when you're asleep, the whole thing lights up." Just as significantly, continues Dr. Schulz, when we are awake our brain's frontal lobe, where judgment and critical thinking take place, is constantly telling us "most things we want to do are ridiculous, so why bother. The frontal lobe is our grand censor. But when we're asleep, it's suppressed."

Parapsychology researcher Rhea White did a survey in 1964 of psi test subjects, those who were the most successful in laboratory experiments, to learn how they willfully entered a psi-receptive state. Reaching a level of deep mental and physical relaxation turned out to be the key, because these psi-gifted people had learned to develop and practice a variety of ritualized techniques to still the mind and body for inducing and enhancing their psi receptivity. Charles Honorton at New York's Maimonides Medical Center similarly found, after examining thirteen experimental studies of psi using induced relaxation exercises, that receptivity had been enhanced "more than a billion to one" beyond chance expectation.

Reading Upton Sinclair's book, *Mental Radio*, about his wife's gift for clairvoyance, I noticed that she had described her psi-receptive state in a way that sounded similar to meditation: "I completely relax the mental hold of, or awareness of, all bodily sensations . . . all mental interest in everything in the environment . . . to make the conscious mind a blank."

Professor Gertrude Schmeidler at City College of New York asked six graduate students in her 1970 experimental psychology course to do a psi experiment before and after receiving instructions in meditation by an Indian swami. None of the students had any prior experience with either meditation or parapsychological experiments. Their psi scores before meditation were at chance expectation. After meditating, their scores shifted "significantly above chance," prompting Schmeidler to call the overall results "quite impressive." A year later, twenty-five people who had been meditating for at least six months were compared to twenty-five students who had never practiced meditation. Their task was to influence the performance of a random number generator. The meditators had fifteen minutes before the experiment to meditate. Their scores, as reported to the American Parapsychological Association, were "significantly superior" to the non-meditators.

Two researchers from Finland conducted an experiment in 1966 that apparently demonstrated an ability to predict some aspects of the future while test subjects were hypnotized. While under hypnosis the participants were asked to intuit in what order the numbers one through ten would be randomly selected the next day, and also to indicate how certain they felt about the accuracy of their prediction.

The next day someone who had not been present when the predictions were made listed the numbers at random on a sheet of paper. Quite remarkably, in those cases where test subjects cited a certainty about their predictions, their number orders matched the target sheet of paper at such a rate as to defy chance expectation by odds of 50 million to one. Was this "mere coincidence?" Classic examples of precognition? Or had the test subjects somehow mentally influenced the number selection process?

Psychiatrist Judith Orloff calls meditation "the most powerful tool I have found to become more psychically attuned. It allows us to cross over boundaries we may not know existed until we've moved beyond them." She believes that most of us are so conditioned to hear only our minds and the overriding intensity of our thoughts that we never realize the extent to which we possess psychic abilities. By quieting the mind, meditation helps to broaden our awareness.

Dream Recall and Luck Enhancement

It has been said that each dream we have is really three dreams in one: the dream we actually experience, the dream we remember, and the dream we tell ourselves and others. As a result of the very human tendency to psychologically edit dreams, resulting in distortions or the displacement of details, many lucky psi dreams, says the University of Virginia's Professor Robert Van de Castle, "may be unnoticed by the dreamer himself if he is not sufficiently attuned to the types of dream imagery he employs to represent certain emotionally pertinent ideas or interactions."

A similar finding was made by Professor Louisa Rhine in her psi experiments at Duke University. Of 3,290 cases of precognition she collected, sixty-eight percent had occurred in a dream state. Rhine was struck by how easily intuitive impressions or psi can be repressed or misinterpreted by our conscious minds. "The impression from inception to consciousness may be deflected along the way, distorted, fragmented, or even quite blocked out of expression," she wrote.

A talented dreamworker I know, Jodi Gold, estimates that five percent of her remembered dreams contain precognitive information. She has also worked with countless precognitive dreams from hundreds of participants in the consciousness workshops she conducts under the auspices of The Pathways Institute, a company she co-owns with another gifted dreamworker, Carole Kammen.

To break down the usual barriers to "knowing" and "seeing" that our egos and personal issues erect, the twelve-day workshops conducted by Jodi and Carole combine early morning dreamwork with meditations, artwork, movement energetics, and periods of silence and fasting. These practices together have the effect, in Jodi's words, of "opening our ability to see fundamental patterns and form, without our personal material getting in the way." The result is a heightened intuitive state that facilitates our experience of premonitions, precognitive dreaming, and gaining access to unusual realms of consciousness.

Many of the dreams inspired in this manner herald major life changes or transitions. Jodi had one of her own years ago while spending the night in Volcano National Park on the big island of Hawaii. "I dreamt that I was wandering around the park and came upon a ritual at the volcano's crater. Native Hawaiians were running from a ritual field to the crater and throwing things into it, things they no longer wanted or needed. The dream was very sensate. It was exciting and thrilling. My heart was beating fast and I was in awe and gratitude that I had come upon this ritual.

"After I awoke the next day, I was wandering through the park and found an area that was literally the sacred space of the park. When I got there, Hawaiian men and women were dancing at the edge of the crater. Their hula teacher had passed away and they were honoring the teacher. They took flowers from around their ankles and threw them over the edge of the crater. This place and these people were exactly what I had seen in my dream. The same feelings of being thrilled and excited came up as in my dream. My heart was beating fast. It was a life-changing, powerful, and important place and moment for me. I was in a transition between relationships, and I was considering becoming a full-time teacher. The dream seemed to have set a course for me."

Luck in Dreams

In his book, *Conscious Dreaming*, and on his Web site (www. mossdreams.com), dreamwork teacher and novelist Robert Moss describes a series of cues you can use to detect possibly precognitive information in dreams.

- Does the location of your dream feel realistic but unfamiliar? You may have glimpsed a future scene in your life.
- Does a letter or phone call or other message appear in your dream? This could be a literal alert to a future news event.
- Does someone from your distant past appear in your dream? This could either mean you will cross paths with this person again, or someone else resembling qualities possessed by this person will enter your life.
- Does the dream message appear more than once in a night? Repetition of dream material often means that our unconscious desperately wants our conscious mind to be aware of something.

On Dr. Arthur Bernard's Web site (www.dreamtechniques.com), he calls dreaming "the inner language of the soul through which wisdom is transmitted to our conscious minds." He teaches a dream "incubation" process in his seminars to enable people to program dream themes and then use their dreams to improve their conscious lives.

A lucky person takes active steps to remember dreams and reflects on their meaning.

Even when precognitive information is absent, dream comprehension helps us to understand our deeper selves, our motivations, our personal issues. This is an important step in creating desirable attitudes and behaviors that help us attract luck.

Lucky people use their intuition while awake to act upon life themes and information generated by their dreams.

Synchronicities and dreams are both symbol-rich experiences. Only intuition can summon the key to unlock their luck secrets.

Lucky people consider their glimpses of the future to be possibilities rather than actualities.

They realize that events large and small can still be shaped, even at the margins, and that luck can sometimes be defined as simply being given the opportunity to emotionally prepare for an eventuality.

PART THREE

CREATING YOUR OWN
GOOD LUCK

CHAPTER 7

The Powers of Attraction

"Each man is the smith of his own fortune."
—Appius Claudius Caecus, 312-279 B.C.

*"When the mind is turned to a particular thought
and dwells on it, a definite vibration of matter is set
up, and the oftener this vibration is caused the more
does it tend to repeat itself, to become a habit."*
—Annie Besant, British philosopher

"Fortune smiles at some, and laughs at some others," says the actor Alan Arkin, playing a burned-out, cynical insurance claims adjuster in the 2002 movie, *13 Conversations About One Thing.* As the movie opens we find Arkin's character in a New York bar conversing with an idealistic assistant city prosecutor, played by Matthew McConaughey, who has just declared to Arkin that "luck is a lazy man's excuse."

Arkin's character proceeds to tell the story of a co-worker at his insurance company who won $2 million in the New York lottery and then had his life fall apart. After quitting his job to enjoy a cushy retirement, the lottery winner was besieged by people wanting money. Even his son tried to extort money from him. His wife demanded her share and then walked out on him. His mother-in-law filed a lawsuit against him claiming that the candle she had lit and the prayer she had uttered for him to win the lottery before the drawing was held entitled her to reap half of the winnings that God had bestowed on him. Arkin relates, with undisguised satisfaction, how the man went broke and came begging for his old job and his old life back.

153

"If there really is luck," the assistant prosecutor replies to Arkin's story, "I hope I am lucky enough to recognize it when it comes my way."

Some of the scenes in this thought-provoking film about luck, fate, and happiness are based on real-life situations. The lawsuit filed by the mother-in-law of a lottery winner, for instance, really happened as it was described. The portrayal of the lottery winner's bankruptcy also rings true.

Consider what happened to Curtis Sharp, a maintenance worker for Bell Labs when he won $5 million in a 1982 New York state lottery drawing. His press conference at the World Trade Center in New York, where he accepted the first of his twenty-one annual payments, was a mob scene of reporters because, for that era in lottery history, his jackpot ranked as one of the largest ever.

This public attention turned Sharp into a poster caricature for the American dream of becoming an instant millionaire. He appeared on television commercials promoting lottery ticket sales, and when he showed up at professional sporting events the crowds cheered him. People tried to get close and shake his hand, or rub up against him on the street in the hope that his luck would literally rub off on them. He was living proof that any common working Joe could strike it rich overnight in the United States of America.

Fifteen years after winning his millions, Curtis Sharp was broke, living in Nashville, Tennessee, preaching to other homeless and destitute men. This former icon of good luck had become a symbol for the dark side of lottery rags-to-riches stories.

The day a co-worker informed him that his ticket matched the winning numbers, Sharp passed out. "I fell right on the floor," he confessed to reporters. "They got me up and put a cigarette in my mouth. I don't even smoke." His $5 million was to be paid out in twenty-one installments of $238,000 a year ($191,000 after taxes).

A year later Sharp got married and spent $100,000 on the wedding. He bought a new Cadillac, a house in New Jersey, and hired a driver and a secretary to help answer the deluge of pleas for money coming from both relatives and strangers. Some of his investments became sinkholes. Sharp lost $60,000 when a financial planner disappeared with investor money, and $219,000 when a tax shelter went under. By 1999 Sharp's entire lottery fortune was gone. He had sold his last few yearly installments to a company that specialized in buying out financially-strapped lottery winners' annual payments at bargain rates.

Sharp's story illustrates a remarkable statistic—*one in every two United States lottery winners eventually gets into serious financial trouble or goes bankrupt*. Similar problems among lottery winners in Britain have been documented in surveys conducted by *The London Telegraph*. In May 2002, an article headlined "When Good Luck Is A Bad Omen" related a series of these hard-luck lottery stories:

- Philip Kitchen won two million pounds (nearly $4 million) in 1999, retired from his job as a master carpenter, and went into seclusion. He became an alcoholic, rarely left his house for months at a time, and died alone less than two years after receiving his windfall.
- Friends Mark Gardiner and Paul Maddison won 22.6 million pounds (over $40 million) in 1996, but they had a falling-out, stopped speaking to each other, and Maddison's own mother disowned him.
- Mukhtar Mohidin got lucky with a lottery jackpot of 17.9 million pounds (nearly $30 million) in 1994, but became overwhelmed with guilt because his Muslim faith forbids gambling. The next year his wife sued him for money and then sued him for divorce after seventeen years of marriage.
- In 1996, Roger Robar collected 6 million pounds (over $10 million) in the lottery. The next year he married a woman twenty years his junior, though she soon left him with their baby after he resisted her family's financial demands. "I've been very lucky with money," Roger confessed to the newspaper, "but unlucky with love."

When lightning in the form of a large fortune strikes, few people are psychologically prepared to handle the consequences. Toxic behaviors and attitudes can quickly flip good luck into misfortune. Going from poverty to wealth, and back to poverty again, often happens because, while the outward circumstances of a winner's life may have changed as a result of luck, his subconscious mind is still programmed with a poverty consciousness. Sometimes he fears success because it is inconsistent with his own low self-image.

By contrast, I have noticed that people with naturally high self esteem seem to have an easier time attracting luck, sustaining good fortune, and flipping a run of bad luck back into good. For a case-book example of how to flip a streak of bad luck, I turned to Greg Peters, formerly in practice as a psychotherapist in Houston, Texas. Misfortune began for Peters innocently enough when he accidentally drove over a curb and knocked the muffler off his automobile, creating an extremely loud and annoying disturbance wherever he went. He had a date that night with a woman he desired a relationship with, but she called and cancelled in a manner that telegraphed to Greg that she didn't want to see him again. These two incidents were the beginning of an intensifying trend of things going wrong in his life.

"It was as if I had entered some sort of zone, a problem zone," he told me. "Every day three or four things out of my control went wrong. Some were very costly. For a solid week the problems were multiplying every day. It quit feeling like accidents. At the time I called it a problem streak rather than a bad luck streak. But I guess they are the same. I felt out of control, as if at any moment something new would hit me. And usually it did. I didn't know what was happening to me. It created a lot of anxiety. It was very unusual and it felt meaningful."

Greg's training and experience as a psychotherapist were useful during this streak of misfortune, enabling him to adopt an observer's point of view and to reflect on the patterns, synchronicities, and lessons that the problems taken together might reveal. "I realized that my tendency had been to get depressed or taken down by anything negative that occurred in my life. In the midst of this downward spiral I pulled out some spiritual readings. I wasn't then affiliated with any particular religion, but I also didn't feel like the universe was entirely random or accidental. I came to believe that everything that was happening to me during this period was a test. Then, with my detachment, I started to develop a sense of humor about it all. It seemed like a big joke or a trick being played on me. Thanks to being able to laugh about it, I began to relax and was much less bothered by the negative events."

His application of good humor and a detached observer frame of mind proved to be the formula of attitude and behavior that broke the bad luck spell. "One morning, I woke up and had the feeling the streak was gone. I woke up and knew it would be a normal day. The clustering of problems was over. And that's exactly what happened. It was over, and in the decade or more since, nothing like it has ever visited my life."

Magic in Everyday Life

As a child, Bill Gladstone was so used to having good luck that he expected it as a normal part of life. By concentrating on cards and dice he seemed able to access a sixth sense about outcomes. This ability proved quite useful in playing Little League baseball, enabling him to anticipate the direction of a ball almost before the bat and ball collided. Later in life, after establishing the successful literary agency Waterside Productions, he attributed his fortune to having "moved into a flow that is entirely supported by the universe."

So what is the key to harnessing that flow? Gladstone elaborates in his book, *Be The Deal*, describing an inner conviction and attitude that shaped, and continues to influence, his life. "At a core level I have always felt that I could generate my own luck and magic. I never felt that long odds alone should dictate whether or not to engage in an activity or enterprise. I expected magic on a daily basis and felt that I had a personal relationship with the keeper of good fortune, and that my primary obligation in order to manifest this good luck was to merely concentrate on my desired results."

For Gladstone the flow is "an underlying power which moves us when we allow it to move us—an intuitively-driven inspiration which is the source of all good luck, insight, and business break-throughs." Besides developing a positive, can-do attitude about everything we attempt in life, Gladstone urges us to open our minds to expect miracles if we want to experience them. But first we must be willing and able to take action to prepare us for good fortune. After all, in the game of golf few if any holes-in-one are made by golfers who do not aim at the hole, nor does anyone win the lottery without first buying a ticket.

Opening up opportunities for luck often depends on opening our minds to the potential that exists around us every day. In this regard, Thomas Jefferson wrote: "I'm a great believer in luck, and I find the harder I work the more I have of it." In college football during the twentieth century, University of Texas coach Darrell Royal, a buddy of country singer Willie Nelson, was fond of de-scribing luck as "what occurs when preparation meets opportunity." It was a phrase he had borrowed from a scientist, Louis Pasteur.

Luck comes fastest and easiest to those people who wish for it, believe they deserve it, expect they will receive it, and work hard to create the opportunities to achieve it. But attracting good luck is also about not being so attached to the outcome that we treat our preferences as if they were addictions.

Creating luck is an attitude about life and a skill anyone can learn. It requires that you use your intuition to "go with the flow," to be willing to discard your belief systems and patterns of behav-ior when they inhibit you, and to remain open to partnering with whatever higher power you believe exists. One of the most remark-able people in this or any epoch of history, Helen Keller, who tran-scended blindness and deafness to become a beacon of hope for the human spirit, wrote this about luck: "When one door closes, an-other opens. But we often look so long and so regretfully at the closed door that we do not notice the one which has opened for us."

In a study on luck performed by several psychologists at England's University of Hertfordshire, one hundred people were surveyed, half of whom considered themselves to be lucky and the other half unlucky. The fifty people who believed themselves lucky were more likely to remember the positive events from their lives and forget the negative, while the so-called "unlucky" people had just the opposite experience with memories. As a result, the study authors concluded that "lucky-thinking" people work more diligently for what they want in life, while people feeling "unlucky" sabotage themselves with pessimism and toxic memories.

An important question about luck to ask yourself involves whether what you want is within reason. Take the state lotteries, which more than half of all Americans have played at least once. Suppose we all had a magic formula for winning. Suppose the 30 million residents of California each played and won, sharing one dollar each from a $30 million jackpot. Very quickly people would stop playing, and those jackpots, and the lotteries themselves, would disappear. It is important for us to realize a key principle of how Lady Luck works: she doesn't necessarily always give us what we want; she often provides us only with what we need.

Getting in Tune with Your Goals

Among those who coach others on ways to achieve their professional and personal goals, the laws of attraction are a widely used process based on the principle that like attracts like. To get what you want in life, to create good luck, you must put yourself in the right alignment, or "vibrational" state of mind, with your goal.

If you say to yourself, "I will be happy when I make a lot of money," observes Dr. Rachna Jain, a clinical psychologist and goal coach based in Columbia, Maryland, "the law of attraction says you must make yourself happy first, which puts you into the vibrational space of attracting the money you want." The attraction laws that Dr. Jain uses with her clients, and which she in turn learned from

Esther Hicks, a teacher in San Antonio, Texas, focus on surfacing and clearing out negative, limiting beliefs. A series of luck-conducting steps are involved.

- Become clear on what it is you DON'T want.
- Become clear on what you DO want.
- Allow yourself to FEEL the joy of possessing what you desire, as if you already possess it.
- Note any inspired ideas or actions that surface when you feel this joy you have summoned.
- Take action on these ideas or thoughts of action.
- Have faith and trust that what you desire is on its way to you.
- Be alert to little proofs providing evidence that what you desire is indeed forthcoming.
- Finally, adopt an "attitude of gratitude" for the appearance of this evidence to help attract the bigger goal more quickly.

"It's good to try this process on small things first," counsels Dr. Jain. "Let's say you want a new watch. You first get clear on what you don't want. I don't want it to be real expensive or hard to get. After making a list of what you don't want, you then make a list of what you do. Then you feel like you've already got the watch, saying how good it looks on your wrist. After the feeling, you use intuition to see what ideas come up on acquiring it. When the indications come up from the universe, the synchronicities of what you are to do next, you then project the attitude of gratitude.

"You can use this process to create more money in your life as long as you get really clear on what having the money will give you. If it's going to bring you joy, you get into a joyful place. Even if you find a penny on the ground, be grateful and playful that you found just a penny and you start to experience more money. I know someone who played this game one entire weekend, trying to see how much money she could find. By the end of the weekend she had found $125, in denominations of up to $20 at a time. It's about creating a more abundant consciousness where you start to see the money you want come in from any source.

"This is a step-by-step process where anyone can become more lucky. I had a client who invoked the process to obtain a leather couch. Soon thereafter, a furniture truck broke down in front of her house. The furniture was unloaded and they left behind just the sort of leather couch she wanted. I've used the process numerous times in my own life. I used it to attract the man I believe I will marry. I made my list of what I did and didn't want, and within weeks he showed up in my life.

"I believe all of our reality is self-created and we have choices in how we see events. I don't believe we're at the mercy of an uncaring universe. If you are always looking for the thousand-dollar bill, you can be blind to the same amount coming to you as one thousand one-dollar bills. We tend to think of things coming to us in a very linear way, as in 'I work hard and get this much in return.' I think the channels of the universal flow are much bigger and diverse. It's our use of intuition that allows us to short-circuit the linear process and access the knowledge of a mass consciousness."

Just as many people have difficulty sitting in the quiet that intuition demands for us to hear it clearly, others grow impatient with adhering to all of the steps of the attraction law. They get stuck by thinking of what they want to create, all the while repeating to themselves a negative, "It's not here yet, it's not here yet." Such negativity takes us out of alignment with the vital belief that what we want is really and truly coming.

Canadian law-of-attraction coach Michael Losier suggests these "tools" to help lessen the doubt. First, identify your desire, then raise the vibration or feeling intensity level around it, and finally allow it to happen. When that little or loud internal voice of doubt speaks up, create statements in your mind or on paper (affirmations) that convincingly make the case that your desire is possible. Writes Losier on his Web site: "Let's say, for example, that your desire is to attract your ideal client, or your ideal relationship, and you have a feeling of doubt that it is possible for you. Your doubt or resistance is what is stopping you from allowing your ideal desire. To lessen that resistance ask yourself this question: 'Is there anyone on the planet that is doing or having what I desire?' If so, then you now know it is possible. Continue building these sorts of statements."

If you visualize yourself as a giant magnet, with the power to attract, you may begin to see the importance of where you direct the attention of your desires and thoughts. So be careful what you think, since this process can just as easily attract the manifestation of your fears as it does your hopes. Coaches in the law-of-attraction process say the stronger and greater the emotions that you attach to what you desire, to what you seek to attract, the faster the goals will manifest. Creating an intense emotional field boosts and amplifies your magnetic attraction powers.

"As a man thinks in his heart, so is he" (Proverbs 23:7). This Biblical admonition is at the "heart" of the law-of-attraction process. It reminds us that if we are indeed a magnet that attracts, the heart is the vibrator of the signals we send out. It also reminds us to remain "lighthearted," to find happiness within, and discover the joy in music, art, children, animals, love, and all endeavors that uplift the human spirit.

The "Magic" of Beginner's Luck

Most of us tend to attach the label of "beginner's luck" to those people who perform a skill or task well the first time they try, because we think their success could only be a result of overcoming their ignorance of the "right" way to conduct themselves. We reason that luck came despite the absence of their experience or training. As I began to study the attitudes and behaviors evident in a variety of beginner's luck cases, including my own eleven-week lucky run as a fledgling gambler, a pattern emerged from the beginners that also seemed present in those lucky people who consistently attract streaks of good fortune.

To illustrate what I mean, let's look at the experience of a management consultant I know, Palen Anderson, whose first attempt to play the game of blackjack yielded a remarkable result. She had gone to the casinos of Atlantic City somewhat reluctantly to appease the wishes of some friends. She sat down at a blackjack table having only a vague familiarity with the rules of play. She won the first hand that was dealt, then the second hand, the third, the fourth, and more, collecting $100 with each win.

"I won nine hands in a row until I intuitively felt I should stop," Palen told me. "I was detached. I didn't know what I was doing. I had no attachment to the outcome. I was just having fun. It was like I had entered a stream and just ran with it. I've been called lucky all of my life, and it's really just moments of grace. I think of luck as moments in time when everything just lines up in your favor."

Have you ever noticed how often a person who knows nothing about sports in general, or about any particular sports teams, wins the office betting pool? In my direct experience, and based on observations from listening to others, I've noticed it happening frequently over the years. While working in a Boston research lab, neuroscientist Mona Lisa Schulz gained a reputation among co-workers as an extraordinary intuitive. She knew nothing about football, yet on Fridays, when she made her professional football picks of winners in the office pool, she usually won.

"I won so often that my colleagues finally eliminated me from the pool," Dr. Schulz wrote in her book, *Awakening Intuition*. "I think the bet that put them over the edge was the time I picked Green Bay, which was 1-11, to win by six points over Dallas, the reigning Super Bowl champs. 'How could you have known that?' my boss demanded sourly as he handed me fifty dollars."

My friend Elizabeth Solliday had a similar experience while still in high school in Chicago. Her boyfriend at the time and several dozen of his buddies had organized a betting pool for the national college basketball tournament. Each person put in $5 and tried to pick the winners among the sixty-four teams that started the tournament playoffs. The boys all laughed at her when she paid $5 and began making her picks, because she was the only girl to enter the she knew nothing about college basketball or about any of the teams.

"I was in a giddy mood. I had this feeling of, why not enter the pool? And of course I would have as much of a chance of winning as anyone. The guys were all arguing the relative merits of each team, and I just tuned them out and made my picks. I used intuition. In five minutes I picked the winners of the games and handed in my list. I had no attachment to the outcome, and I had a sense of playfulness about it all. At the end of the tournament, I had picked the most winners and won the $500 pot. All the guys were mad at me. They wanted to know how I did it. They kept calling it beginner's luck."

Later in life, Elizabeth got her master's degree in psychology and developed an informed perspective on what beginner's luck really means. "It feels like unknowingly tuning in to a higher stream of consciousness. There's a presumptuousness about it and an unspoken trust. When streaks of luck have occurred in my life, it feels like what I experienced with beginner's luck. I'm aware that I'm in a stream and I consciously shake off any conflicts or doubts to sustain the streak. It's not a discriminative process. And I find the capacity to remember positive events is important as a reinforcement. It's a sort of building up of a bank account of positive memories to reinforce the sense of trust that enables me to discount the moments of doubt. There is no mental activity. It's all spontaneous."

Summoning a positive "beginner's" mind proved immensely beneficial to Liza Gutierrez-O'Neill, a 31-year-old public relations executive from south Florida, when she gambled for the first time. Along with her husband and a group of friends, Liza spent four nights in Las Vegas and tested her luck on quarter slot machines and the craps tables. She described her experiences to me.

"I mentally kept repeating to myself, 'I am lucky. I have the power to succeed at anything I try.' It helped me focus on what I am in control of and what God is in control of. I went as far as dressing the part, dressing like I had money, with the hope it would help attract money to me. Somehow it did. I won on both slots and dice. I only played at dice tables that generated a fun spirit, with people laughing, cheering, and having a positively good and fun time. One gentleman rolled nine times and each time rolled a winning seven. When I felt comfortable enough to play, I followed the rollers who were on a hot streak. I accumulated $245 in winnings while saying to myself, 'If it is meant to be, then so be it. All that I want is all I can be.' I budgeted $20 a day for playing the quarter slots. I played the maximum of three quarters in each machine. I never stayed at a machine for more than five plays."

Liza won big on the slot machines and left Las Vegas with $2,500 more than she arrived with. The next year she returned with the same group of people and once again used the process of positive thinking. This time she left with $1,650 in winnings, mostly from slots. Her husband, Chris, commented to her after the inaugural trip how "most people win their first time in Vegas." His remark illustrates a widespread perception that beginner's luck is a common phenomenon. But if it is indeed so frequent, why is that so? Shouldn't this frequency, in theory, violate the law of averages?

Qualities of beginner's luck, those attitudes and behaviors that usually accompany its occurrence, are relatively easy to identify and provide us with clues to the secret of how luck is created and sustained. There is an openness, an excitement, playfulness, positive thoughts, a lack of judgment or concern about failure, and little or no attachment to the outcome. All of these attributes taken together create a vibrant, open channel through which intuition flows unconstrained by inhibiting structures normally active in the rational mind.

"In life, if you focus on possibilities, they become probabilities," observes neuroscientist Mona Lisa Schulz. "How you perceive the world and everything in it affects how the world influences you."

A Secret of Money-Luck Karma

Though only nine years old at the time, Uriel Dana sensed that something meaningful had happened to her, one of life's periodic big lessons that would help shape her destiny. An older couple who were friends of her family had taken her to one of their church functions in Chicago. It was called a cakewalk. Everyone paid a nickel and went to stand in a square on a large, bingo-type board spread on the floor. If your square was drawn, you won a cake. Uriel won the first cake and immediately gave it to the couple who had brought her. Then she won a second cake, and a third cake, giving each away to people at random. She kept the fourth cake for herself.

"Wow," Uriel marveled, "I'm just lucky wherever I stand!"

This serendipitous good fortune became a common feature of her life. At age twenty, she and three girlfriends saved their money and went on a three-day tour to Denmark. The hotel where they stayed gave each of them a single token to play in a slot machine. Uriel's token won her $400, all of which she spent on her friends, buying them meals and a night at the opera.

Trained as an engineer, Uriel became successful in that profession, but her heart's desire was to be a painter. While living in West Germany, she made the decision to switch professions and in 1984 became the apprentice, then the fulltime painting partner, and later the intimate partner, of internationally known painter Gage Taylor. Due to an accident, Taylor's ex-wife had become disabled, and he was financially strapped as a result of helping to pay for her medical care. Uriel shared her savings with him, as well as money from the sale of her automobile.

She fantasized about eventually owning a nice car, specifically a white BMW 500 series with a sunroof. Whenever she saw someone driving that make of car, she wished it for herself, but she also wished something better for the other driver. That practice was the foundation of her win/win attitude about luck and prosperity. Uriel soon saw her wish about the car fulfilled in an unexpected fashion.

"Gage and I were having dinner with another couple at their home. They were about to move to the south of France. The man's name was Joseph, a well-known international painter who had married a friend of ours. Out of nowhere, Joseph said to me, 'God told me to give you my car.' He had decided to give it to me rather than sell it before moving. He signed it over to me. It was a white BMW 500 series with a sunroof. Exactly what I had been secretly wanting."

If indeed it is true that givers gain most when they least expect to, or don't expect to, then Uriel must have accumulated good money karma because the fortuitous trend in her fortunes continued. "We were at a party and met a psychiatrist who owned one of Gage's prints called 'The Secret Of Life.' The wife and I were talking and she said, 'You look really tired—what's going on with you?' I explained some of the stress in our lives and she said, 'You need a vacation. Where would you like to go?' Playing along, I said Maui. Then she and her husband said, 'Okay, we want to send the two of you there.' And they did. They paid for our airfare, hotel, and rental car."

"On our second day in Maui, Gage and I were driving to Hana in the rain and we saw a black sand beach. We stopped and I felt guided to this one area of the deserted beach. Something caught my eye in the sand. It was a tiny burgundy triangle sticking out of the black sand. I stuck my hand in and pulled out this big wad of cash. Three hundred and eighty-nine dollars! With a burgundy wrap around it. No identification. Just cash in the sand and no one around. That paid for all of our meals on the trip. I felt the universe saying *yes*!

"When we came back home we were broke. That's how artists live. Feast to famine. We were driving on a lane near a state park and I slammed on the brakes and jumped out of the car. It was four in the afternoon and Gage thought I'd gone nuts. This redhead running wildly in the street. I had seen these green wads of paper blowing around and a voice inside of me had said, 'Go get it right now!' It was money. Eighty-seven dollars that bought us groceries and gas just when we most needed it."

Uriel's pattern of synchronistic luck not only continued, it seemed to intensify. She and Gage lived in a carriage house behind a larger house in San Rafael, California. The main house was occupied by a couple who didn't like reading, yet who had inherited stacks of books from the previous owner. Uriel picks up the story. "We needed to move someplace with more acreage because we had been given two sheepdogs. We found a place but we were two thousand, four hundred dollars short on what we needed to move in, to pay the security deposit, and first and last months' rent. The couple in the main house had told us we could take whichever books we wanted before they discarded them. We started going through them and realized they were all first editions. Some were first editions signed by the authors—Robert Frost and W. Somerset Maugham. We sold them at a rare-book store and got two thousand, four hundred dollars for them. It was exactly what we needed to move."

Does Uriel have a recipe for success? Is a law of attraction at work in her favor? She has some definite ideas. "I think luck is when you align your energy at the right time, in the right way, with the right intention, and things just come to you. Spirit honors the good work that we do. When you're not getting enough, no matter what it is—money, love—you need to give more of the same. And always keep an attitude of gratitude."

From what I know of her, Uriel is also almost unerringly tapped into the clairvoyant channel of her own intuition. She has sharpened that faculty by practicing Tibetan dream yoga techniques and studying the world's religions, mythologies, and archetypes. Since Gage's death in 2000, she has continued her emergence as a remarkable talent. Her unique paintings of fantastical scenes reflect the depth of this lucky woman's transcendent spirit.

Some people just seem to have a natural money-luck karma. Stan Gooch in England is another who comes to mind. As Gooch explains, "All my adult life I seem to have had the knack of attracting unearned income, and especially when matters were desperate." Each week Gooch would find at least $10 at a time lying on the streets and sidewalks of London. Eventually, Gooch came to believe that he had money-luck karma, and that belief seemed to magnetize the process even more in a sort of self-fulfilling prophecy.

Does Belief Affect Luck?

"Belief is a potent factor in the expression of consciousness," declared the late Alan Vaughan, a gifted intuitive who wrote *Incredible Coincidence* and other books. "Those who believe in ESP score above chance on ESP tests; those who disbelieve score below chance. In life, this could be translated into: We get what we believe we will get. Miracles mostly happen to those who believe in miracles."

As if to underscore Vaughan's point, I came across a fascinating study conducted in 1996 by five psychologists from three British universities, examining how people classified as lucky or unlucky performed on a psi test. Experimental subjects, fifty-six undergraduates at the University of Hertfordshire, responded to a questionnaire in which each participant guessed the outcomes of fifty computer-generated coin-flips. Before undertaking this task they were asked to predict how well they felt they would perform. "The better the subjects thought they would do at guessing the outcomes of the coin-flips," concluded the study authors, "the better they actually did." Belief truly did appear to shape outcomes!

In 1968 two psychologists at UCLA tested the idea that people who believe in psi score higher on psi tests than those who are skeptical. With 144 volunteers, male and female, ranging in age from fourteen to sixty-five, three groups of test subjects were formed. The psi group was composed of twenty-four pairs of people who believed they had experienced ESP. Group two was twenty-four pairs who didn't believe they had experienced ESP, but who were open to its existence. The third group of pairs all expressed the conviction that ESP didn't exist.

One member of each pair was placed in a soundproof room and shown a series of colored slides on particular themes. This person attempted to transmit these images or associated feelings to a partner in another room, who recorded his or her impressions into a tape recorder. Those in the ESP believer group scored accurately, with a probability of one in 3,000 against the results being the product of chance, while the other two groups scored at chance expectation. Additional experiments found that creative people (writers, painters, musicians, etc.) consistently scored above chance on the same test, while other professional groups failed to exceed chance expectation.

By evaluating wellness studies and conducting his own investigations, Dr. Herbert Benson, an associate professor of medicine at Harvard Medical School, came to the firm conclusion that our expectations and beliefs have direct physical repercussions. We can literally program ourselves at the cellular level to mimic what our minds either desire or fear.

That old adage "be careful what you wish for" has documented effects on the human body, especially regarding pregnancy. "Women, and in rare cases men, who either desired or feared pregnancy, or empathized with someone who was pregnant, have been known to show actual signs of pregnancy," writes Dr. Benson in his book, *Timeless Healing.* One of the more famous cases cited was Mary Tudor, a sixteenth-century queen of England, whose pregnancy symptoms—including abdominal swelling and cessation of menstruation—lasted nine months and culminated with false labor.

Because our brains can't always distinguish between externally and internally created reality, and we are literally wired for responses to our expectations and beliefs, some remarkable effects can occur that defy conventional cause-and-effect medical explanations. "When activated, the body can respond as it would if the belief were a reality, producing deafness or thirst, health or illness," says Dr. Benson.

A report appeared in *Clinical Psychology Review* in 1994, describing a study which concluded that seventy percent of patients examined had experienced excellent results in recovery from asthma and certain types of ulcers after being given a placebo instead of real medicine. Their "condition of heightened expectations" about being cured had succeeded in activating their mind-body connection in a way that cured them without the need for actual drug intervention.

Since, as Dr. Benson points out, "our everyday thoughts, dreams, and superstitions" intimately affect every aspect of our physical selves, is it really such a leap to suppose that our beliefs and expectations might influence other aspects of physical reality? A clue about the possible mechanism comes from neurologist Richard Cytowic, whose book, *The Man Who Tasted Shapes*, makes a case that most of us have lost many brain abilities that evolution had given our species. "If you want to try to reclaim some of this deeper knowledge," wrote Dr. Cytowic, "I suggest that you start with emotion, which to me seems to reside at the interface between that part of self that is accessible to awareness and that part which is not."

Psychologist Gertrude Schmeidler theorized a half-century ago that psi skeptics, because of the emotional intensity of their negative beliefs, may not consciously have psi experiences because they reflexively repress or avoid them. To test that idea, a Scottish psychologist did a meta-analysis in 1993 of seventy-three published psi experiments involving 4,500 participants, and found psi believers performed better than psi skeptics on the tests with odds greater than *one trillion to one*. Once again, we find evidence for the power of belief to shape our experiences and our interactions with consensus reality.

Luck as a Learnable Skill

Wall Street's premier investment thinker of the twentieth century, Benjamin Graham, in his classic work, *The Intelligent Investor*, said in reference to investors that he had observed, "One lucky break may count for more than a lifetime of journeyman efforts. . . . Behind the luck there must usually exist a background of preparation and disciplined capacity."

Can luck-generating skills, those attitudes and behaviors that mold character and fortunes, actually be taught to anyone? Professor Richard Wiseman, a psychologist at the University of Hertfordshire, and an author of the belief and psi study that I cited earlier, spent a decade investigating, in his words, "the impact on people's lives of chance opportunities, lucky breaks, and being in the right place at the right time." He wanted to know why some people are luckier than others and whether the less lucky could be taught how to become more so. Four hundred volunteers, ranging from 18 to 84 years of age, completed diaries, questionnaires, intelligence tests, and a series of experiments that Dr. Wiseman devised. The results were interesting.

A long list of "unlucky" behaviors emerged from the experiences of people classified as unlucky. These people generally evidenced more tension than lucky people, which to Dr. Wiseman indicated that anxiety disrupts a person's ability to notice unexpected luck opportunities. Unlucky people also miss chance opportunities because the harder they focus on something they desire, the less they actually see alternative possibilities for accomplishing the goal. Unlucky people tended to be locked into unvarying routines, usually failed to follow their intuition, and often dwelled on their past misfortunes.

In a 2003 book based on his research, *The Luck Factor* (not to be confused with Max Gunther's 1973 book of the same title), Dr. Wiseman described four principles that lucky people display to create good fortune:

(1) They use networking, a relaxed attitude about life, and an openness toward new experiences to enhance their skills of noticing or creating chance opportunities.

(2) By meditating and clearing their minds of extraneous thoughts, lucky people are able to listen to their intuitive hunches and make more effective decisions.

(3) Lucky people persist despite failures, and create positive dynamics in their interactions with others, generating expectations for themselves about good fortune that become self-fulfilling.

(4) By not dwelling on misfortune and always reminding themselves how situations could have been worse, lucky people transform bad luck streaks into good luck streaks.

One of Dr. Wiseman's clever tests of his volunteer subjects involved having groups of both lucky and unlucky individuals spend a month acting out those thoughts and behaviors that Wiseman had identified for lucky people. This exercise helped both groups to recover more quickly from bad luck, listen to their intuition, identify chances for luck more readily, and to have a greater belief and expectation attached to being lucky.

"The results were dramatic," reported Wiseman. "Eighty percent of these people were now happier, more satisfied with their lives and, perhaps most important of all, luckier. While lucky people became luckier, the unlucky had become lucky." Under the auspices of his own research group, The Luck Project (www.luckfactor.co.uk), Dr. Wiseman continues his research into the origin and nature of luck and the psychological edge we can employ to enhance it.

One of the most powerful tools I have encountered to help activate a belief system around luck involves creative visualizations. These "visions of the possible" are a practice of producing mind pictures that act like magnets designed to attract what we need or desire. Harvard Medical School Professor Herbert Benson recommends combining the use of visualizations with affirmations, those positive messages that are repeated over time, because both techniques "introduce a new sensory idea into your brain, especially (if) your brain is accustomed to a stream of negative thoughts or self-criticisms."

Austrian-born actor Arnold Schwarzenegger credits visualization exercises begun in childhood for his success as a bodybuilder and actor. Cartoonist Scott Adams, creator of the Dilbert cartoon series, has ascribed his success to affirmations that he began practicing in childhood. In the next chapter we will examine some of these and other techniques for altering your vibratory relationship to your own vision of leading a lucky life.

What Lucky People Know

"Each of us carves his destiny in the raw clay of chance," the sculptor Rodin once said. Playing the hand we are dealt wisely is sometimes more important than fate having dealt us a winning hand. But, at the same time, it is often said that whatever you fear most in life will eventually get you. The Bible makes the same point: "For what I fear comes upon me, and what I dread befalls me" (Job 3:25).

Professional horse race bettor and newspaper columnist Andrew Beyer makes a similar point about negative thoughts. "Luck can change the course of your life. You can't allow yourself to get unhinged by the bad luck that occurs, because a negative frame of mind feeds on itself."

An engineer who helped design the Apollo spacecraft, Will Munson, wrote a book, *How Lucky Can You Get?*, in which he counseled that for us to gain control over luck in our lives we must be willing to give up our present mental picture of ourselves because "your behavior is not determined by reality, but by your perception of reality." I have also heard this idea expressed with the phrase, "all experience is created internally."

Other fundamental principles of good fortune emerged during my interviews with both lucky and unlucky people: toxic thinking attracts bad luck, but bad luck can be flipped, or turned around into positive experiences. Most unlucky people are not this way just because of unfortunate circumstances. Most unlucky people are paralyzed by anger, cynicism, despair, and an unforgiving attitude that makes them feel like victims, blinding them to opportunities and the everyday magic of life. Inviting good luck into your life often means taking risks, being willing to go beyond your comfort zone.

Lucky people realize that "you are what you think," so they carefully and mindfully cultivate positive thoughts.

Lucky people tend to get over their disappointments much faster than unlucky people.

Lucky people know that luck is attracted to conditions and environments we ourselves can create.

Feeling lucky often translates into *being* lucky. Lucky people look forward to the future with faith and optimism, accentuate the positive in the present, and remember more of the good moments than the bad events from the past.

Most lucky people who have found and kept their soulmates or lifemates did so after first exorcising their own toxic behaviors and attitudes, a process that enabled them to more accurately decipher the synchronicities and intuitive whisperings that eventually brought them into relationship.

Lucky people take the initiative; they don't simply wait for good luck to find them, they take positive steps to attract it.

Lucky people are open to new experiences and embrace change because with it comes new opportunities.

For twenty years former *Time* magazine editor Max Gunther made a practice of asking this question in evaluating the people he encountered: "What do lucky people do that unlucky people don't do?" Gunther came to the conclusion that, in general, "The luckiest men and women are those who have adopted certain approaches to life and have mastered certain kinds of internal psychological manipulations." He noticed five characteristics they had in common, a pattern of attitudes and behaviors that he called the Luck Adjustment:

(1) Lucky people have a knack for initiating friendly contacts with others, creating a sort of magnetic field that is inviting and comfortable. "The bigger your web of friendly contacts, the better the odds in your favor."

(2) Lucky people possess the capacity to generate accurate hunches, and then to act on them. Lucky people can tell the difference between good hunches and the bad ones that are wishes in disguise.

(3) Lucky people tend to be bold people, but not rash, while those who describe themselves as unlucky are often passive and afraid of change.

(4) Lucky people "have the capacity to get out of deteriorating situations quickly. They know how to discard bad luck before it becomes worse luck."

(5) Lucky people are generally happy, but they're not necessarily optimists. They nurture a healthy pessimism in the sense that they are always ready for the worst to happen.

CHAPTER 8

Spiritual Practices That Lead to Success

"The more you know, the more luck you will have."
—Confucius (551-479 B.C.)

"When I pray, coincidences happen; when I don't, they don't."
—Anglican Archbishop William Temple

The night before Doug and Maureen Baldwin won nearly $14 million in the Illinois state lottery in 1996, Maureen made a personal commitment to tithe ten percent of her income every month to her church, something she had never done before. The next day they bought a lottery ticket with selections based on Doug's system of drawing numbers from a hat. As they did before every lottery drawing, they fantasized about what it would be like to win and how they would use the money.

"We usually got our money's worth just sharing our daydreams," says Maureen. "Another real plus for us was that we learned indirectly what we each valued. I would start my list of ideas by saying, 'After the ten percent that I give back to God, I'm going to . . .'. When Doug expressed his ideas on how he would spend the money, he would usually have a plan to help someone in his family."

During his years of playing the lottery in tiny Freeport, Illinois, when asked by friends what he would do with the money if he won, Doug invariably replied, *"If* we win? It's not *if* we win, it's *when* we win!"* It would be a mistake to think this confidence was simply what one should expect from a retired high school track coach. Doug truly felt like a winner.

Maureen describes her and her husband's outlook on life this way. "The most influential aspect of winning is your attitude. Be prepared for something good to happen to you. Anticipate the day when good fortune will come your way. Think and dream about what you will do when it happens. What do you value most in life? What hidden talent or talents do you have that you can share with others? Start sharing them now. If you have nothing more to give than some of your time, start giving some of it away to someone who needs a helping hand. Give without expecting anything in return. In our case, God found us worthy of the stewardship of great wealth."

Former actor and taxi driver Eric Leek of North Arlington, New Jersey, was just 26 years old when he won the 1976 Bicentennial Lottery in his state. His ticket was chosen from 63 million tickets for a payout of $92,000 a year for life. He later told an interviewer that he had always felt lucky, and the day before the drawing he had a strong intuitive feeling he would win. His girlfriend, Tillie, had a precognitive dream several weeks before the drawing in which Eric won "a fantastic amount of money." Leek confessed that his views about luck were mystical. "I believe good luck comes to people who are ready for it and will use it unselfishly to help others. There's a reason for everything that happens, even if we can't always see the reason. There are patterns." Leek used some of his winnings to open a center for troubled youths so his own good luck could "be turned into good luck for some kids I haven't met yet."

Our rational minds may balk at the thought, but a spiritual connection does seem to exist between gambling and grace, a word we use to denote divine assistance, or a special favor from God. When we pray for miracles to happen, we are appealing for good luck graced with grace. "The notion of grace as a kind of spiritual luck, a free gift from God, lies at the heart of gambling's larger cultural significance," writes Rutgers University historian Jackson Lears, in his book *Something for Nothing: Luck in America*.

Grace appears in many secular forms, continues Professor Lears, such as the "oneness with the cosmos that athletes experience when they are 'in the zone,' artists when they are compelled by inspiration, or gamblers when they are on a hot streak. If we are lucky, grace could be what happens when we take a chance, when we cease trying to control events and simply play." Let's consider some more cases of luck appearing as answered prayers, generosity flowing from grace, and the animating belief system that Lears refers to as our "reverence for grace, luck, and fortune—powers beyond human mastery whose favor may nonetheless be courted."

Luck As Poetic Justice

For months, every night before going to sleep, 26-year-old Pam Hiatt recited a prayer asking God to show her a way out of her mounting financial difficulties. "I'm not asking to win the lottery," she would say. "I just need an opportunity so I can afford a little studio apartment."

She was single and eight months pregnant, juggling two part-time jobs while attending college, and had been forced to move in with her parents in Idaho until she could afford a place of her own. About once a week she would purchase a Powerball lottery ticket at a convenience store. She always picked numbers corresponding to the current ages of her mother, sister, three brothers, and herself.

On Saturday, June 4, 1995, Pam bought her ticket, almost changing one of the numbers because her youngest brother had his birthday the previous week. At the last moment, on a whim, or an intuitive hunch, she decided to play the LOTTO card she had already filled out, using his old birthday number. When the twenty-state Powerball drawing was held later that night, Pam won $87.5 million, allotted in twenty annual payments of $4.3 million each.

Seventeen days after winning, Pam gave birth to a son, Nicholas. The studio apartment she had prayed for became a ranch house. This young millionaire mom then set up a charitable foundation to channel donations to the Red Cross and her other favorite causes. "I've been so blessed," Pam told the *Ladies' Home Journal*.

As I researched Pam's story and those of dozens of other lottery winners, a pattern began to emerge. Extraordinary luck in the form of "chance" jackpots often seemed to follow in the wake of hardship and tragedy. Here are a few other illustrations.

- During 1990 and 1991, Angela Thomas lived under a thundercloud of misfortune in Belvedere, South Carolina. She went through a wrenching divorce, suffered a nervous breakdown, and experienced the deaths of both her mother and father. Then, as if to make amends, fate handed the 38-year-old woman a $9 million lottery prize.

- Mary Champaigne underwent her own epic streak of misfortune in Los Angeles. In 1997 her 24-year-old son had been killed by a stray bullet when he happened to be in the wrong place as a gang shootout erupted. Her father and mother-in-law both died the next year. The company where she worked as a personnel trainer went out of business. A month after losing her job, her husband died of cancer. Mary struggled to survive the grief and financial hardship by taking a job in a Starbucks coffee shop. Less than a year later, Mary won more than $6 million in the California lottery.

- Carolyn Hasan was 29 years old when a truck smashed into her car in Ohio and put her into a coma. Her parents, Ernest and Lucille Hasan of Lorain, Ohio, couldn't afford to bring Carolyn home and give her the constant care she needed. Ernest worked as a maintenance man and money was scarce. They were forced to put Carolyn in a nursing home. In August 1999, the couple won an $8 million jackpot in Ohio's lottery, enabling them to bring their daughter home. "The money gave us some peace of mind," declared the 62-year-old Mrs. Hasan.

- Sixty-four-year-old Bonnie Foster of Gun Barrel, Texas, got devastating news in early 2002. Her 38-year-old son, Virgil, had been diagnosed with pancreatic cancer. Unless he got specialized treatment, which insurance wouldn't cover, he would die. Bonnie was a child of the Depression and of parents who were sharecroppers. She had known poverty all her life, but she never lost her faith, and she believed in miracles. On April 6, 2002, not long after her son's diagnosis, Bonnie won $34 million in the Texas lottery. "Now my son won't have to worry about his medical bills," she declared.

- While in his forties, Sundel "Sonny" Judson, a New Jersey traveling salesman, was diagnosed with leukemia and doctors gave him slim odds of living more than a few months. With that death sentence handed down, Judson decided to experience life as if every day were his last. His health remained stable and he earned an impressive amount of money over the ensuing years, much of which he gave away through annual, anonymous donations to a range of charitable organizations. In July 2002, now 73 years old and semi-retired, he won a $165 million jackpot in the New Jersey lottery. "I have been quite fortunate in my life," he told reporters. "I only graduated from high school but I had a job that I loved doing. I have a wonderful wife and family and my health. I've been very lucky. I guess I beat the odds."

My curiosity about this recurring pattern linking hardship and tragedy with a subsequent reaping of good fortune prompted me to visit Konocti Vista and other Indian casinos in my area when they held drawings to give away new vehicles and other prizes. I wanted to see the faces of the winners and learn whether any of them had experienced sustained streaks of good or bad fortune. (Okay, I confess. I also went because I had tickets in the barrel for two of those drawings, and you had to be present to win. On Halloween at Konocti, my name got selected for one of the $500 cash prizes.)

One pattern that quickly surfaced during these drawings was that of repeat winners. At Twin Pines Casino, the man who won a Harley-Davidson motorcycle the night I was in attendance happened to be the same man who had won a Harley-Davidson motorcycle in the previous Twin Pines drawing just a few months earlier. After his name was announced, I heard people in the audience mumbling about how the drawing must have been rigged for someone to "be that damn lucky."

Before a Sunday evening drawing at Konocti for a new 2002 Ford Ranger pickup, there was a series of giveaways of various amounts of cash. A 59-year-old real estate agent named Faye Barulich had her name called for a $250 prize. I noticed that she was crying when she reached the stage, and these weren't tears of joy.

"I came here to win the truck," Faye tearfully told Gloria, Konocti's mistress of ceremonies for the event.

"But you're still eligible to win if you have more tickets," Gloria replied. To which Faye nodded because, as she would later tell me, she realized that she had eleven ticket stubs in the barrel. (Tickets were accumulated by members of the casino's player's club according to how much money they had played in previous months.)

An hour later, Gloria, who had previously been employed by Fitzgerald's Casino in Reno, climbed back onto the stage for the truck drawing, as a uniformed security guard tumbled the large barrel filled with ticket stubs around and around. He reached in among the 10,000 or so stubs, pulled one out, and handed it to Gloria. Her face visibly flushed at the sight of the name handwritten on the stub.

Not far from the stage, Faye Barulich was sitting at a slot machine, idly popping in coins, when she heard Gloria remark into the microphone, "This is her lucky night." At that instant, Faye had a premonition of winning. She was already out of her seat by the time Gloria called her name. This time her tears truly were tears of joy.

As I later learned, the previous two years of Faye's life had been a nightmarish bout with personal tragedy. Her son and her husband had died, just months apart. With their passing, life lost much of its meaning for her. Now, by winning the grand prize, and defying the odds by winning twice in one night, and all during the week of her 60th birthday, Faye had received an affirmation from life, God, fate, or whatever you choose, that the worst was over.

We can always read too much meaning into patterns, especially if we are scanning the event horizon for them, but I have found patterns to be a useful measure of broader themes that animate our collective experience. Hardship morphing into good fortune, as exemplified by the foregoing examples, qualifies as one such theme. Generosity that attracts the blessings of good fortune is another.

Andrew Whittaker Jr. of West Virginia and Thomas Henderson of Texas have more in common than they know. Both are in their mid-fifties, both won the lottery, both are generous by nature, and both were already millionaires when they won. Whittaker made his first fortune as president of three construction companies that build sewage plants and other water projects. Henderson earned his first fortune as a linebacker for the Dallas Cowboys and played in three Super Bowls during the 1970s.

On Christmas Day 2002, Whittaker won the world's largest lottery jackpot for a single ticketholder, $314.9 million in the 23-state Powerball Lottery. He took the money in a lump sum payment of $170 million before taxes. He was not a regular lottery player, but he had bought $100 worth of tickets because the jackpot had gotten so high. His first act on winning was to publicly pledge ten percent as a donation to three church pastors for distribution to the needy. "Seventeen million dollars in the state of West Virginia will really do good for the poor," Whittaker declared.

Henderson also purchased $100 in lottery tickets, his ritual any time the Texas jackpot went over $20 million. In March 2000, this purchase paid off with a winning ticket worth $28 million. His first act on winning was to publicly pledge to build an athletic field in an impoverished neighborhood of East Austin. He had already built a football field and supported a variety of other charitable causes. "I always knew I was going to win the lottery," Henderson told the *Austin American-Statesman*. "I am just going to continue to do the charities that I do."

While I certainly don't believe you must endure hardship and suffering, or always be charitable and saintly, to qualify as a candidate for winning a lottery jackpot, I do sense a theme of generosity and poetic justice in these and other stories that I have heard. The following account may help to put this theme into sharper focus.

A Mother's Wisdom

During my two decades living and working as a journalist in Washington, D.C., I counted among my closest friends the entrepreneur James Davidson, and his younger brother by four years, Dennis. Tall, lanky and athletic, a Cary Grant lookalike, James came as close to being a genuine Renaissance Man as anyone I had ever known. While still a college student he started a national organization, the National Taxpayer's Union, which grew into a force in American politics. He co-wrote a series of international bestselling books on investment and macro-economics. He owned an investment newsletter, co-owned an advertising and publishing company, and later became a global entrepreneur with major holdings in banks, resorts, and other enterprises in New Zealand and Argentina.

Beyond his obvious intelligence and talents, James has always radiated an intangible quality, a power of attraction, that brought him extraordinary luck and helped turn him into a multimillionaire. As I reflect back, I realize that one of the secrets of his success, perhaps the origin of his luck, can be found in his relationship to his mother. I met her several times at her waterside home in Chalk Point, Maryland. Despite having been bedridden with paralysis since the 1950s, Mrs. Davidson maintained a buoyant, indomitable spirit that impressed and inspired me and everyone who knew her. She also seemed to project her life force in ways that mere intuition cannot adequately explain. I recently asked James to talk about luck and the gifts displayed by his mother (who passed away in 2002), and he kindly obliged with these observations.

"My late mother's example and counsel have informed my attitude about luck, as about so much. Unhappily, only recently has what she taught me come into articulate focus. I recall, particularly, a conversation we had last summer (2001). A cousin of hers had died and left her some thousands of dollars. At that time I was struggling to generate enough cash flow to pay for her round-the-clock care (up to $3,000 per week), along with alimony payments to my ex-wife, my mortgage payments, and more. In any event, my costs were staggering.

"So when my mother received the windfall that would have paid her caregivers and other costs for a while, I expected to be able to breathe a little easier. But no sooner did she get the money than she turned around and gave it all away, mostly to one of my nieces to buy a new car, but also to Indian orphans, disabled veterans, Braille books for the blind, and a whole sweep of kind-head causes. I am ashamed to say it, but I was furious. I did not understand how she could be so insensitive to my struggles to make ends meet. She blandly stated that it wasn't a problem because I was blessed with good luck. 'Don't worry,' she told me. 'You will find a way. Whatever you require will be forthcoming. You must believe!'

"What she said could have been sheer, senile idiocy. Or divine wisdom. At the time, I thought the former. But in retrospect, I suspect that she was trying to get me to understand something important about the primacy of the mind and spirit in determining outcomes. I was in Texas recently meeting with an inventor who has more patents than I have shoes. He said something very similar. I think that there is something to it. In my mother's case, I was the instrument of her luck. Being physically immobilized and on life support for the last fifteen years of her life, she had hyper-developed her sensibilities about the less ponderable aspects of life. This came to the fore emphatically in the days before my brother Dennis's death. My mother dreamed that he would die on the 12th of March. For that reason, she strongly counseled me to spend the day with him before I went to Argentina in early March of 1995. On the 12th I returned to my hotel to find an urgent message. Dennis had died of a heart attack while out jogging on that very day, as my mother had predicted to me.

"Most people treat religion as an airy-fairy thing, not to be taken seriously except by grim fanatics. My mother's view was different.

She did not believe that God's miracles were all reserved for people who lived thousands of years ago in the Middle East. Mother believed the Grace of God was alive and real in the here and now. It is what enabled her to survive forty-nine years of paralysis and fifteen years on a ventilator. She died with the full conviction that her spirit would soar when it was no longer confined by the faltering biochemistry of her body. When she died there was a rich collection of contributions filled in to support orphans, starving Indians, and other charitable causes.

"She always sought to convince me that money laid out to help those who couldn't help themselves would be returned, with compound advantage. 'Just believe, it will work.' It was a gift she tried to share with me particularly—making everyone better than he was. With her, charity was in some way a key to blessings."

Luck Can Be Whatever You Need

On the morning of her 35th birthday Annette Annechild awoke and sat bolt upright in bed, feeling startled and scared. Her intuitive voice was telling her, "You have to change your life or you will die." In response her rational mind was recoiling with, "Change my life! Why?"

By most standards, Annette already led a charmed existence. She had been an actress in New York, wrote and published seven books on food and fitness, appeared twice as a guest on *The Oprah Winfrey Show*, had lived in the south of France, and was now married to the wealthy vice president of a Fortune 500 company. Yet, she couldn't ignore this inner voice because her intuition had never failed her.

The voice spoke up again. "You've written everything you know, and you're not in love with your husband."

Annette knew these were truths she had resisted confronting before. "Then what will I do?" she countered.

"You're going to become a therapist," came the reply.

To her rational mind the notion of obtaining a degree and a license as a professional counselor seemed to pose insurmountable barriers. To begin with, she had never even finished college. But later that day, trusting in the guidance of her higher self, she made a series of phone calls, and immediately doors began to open and her fortunes multiplied. Within a year she had ended her unhappy marriage, finished her undergraduate degree, and begun work on her master's. By the age of 42, she had a doctorate and a thriving practice as a therapist in Malibu, California.

Annette eventually moved to Washington D.C., where she decided to pursue a dream of creating a healing arts center, bringing together in one place psychologists, acupuncturists, massage therapists, and other types of healing practitioners. She wanted to situate the center in Georgetown, one of Washington's more fashionable neighborhoods, but the real estate prices seemed out of her reach. Then synchronicity and luck intervened on her behalf.

One night Annette read an inspirational book that advised its readers to conduct an exercise. She was to treat the very next person she encountered as if he or she were God. That person turned out to be a surly woman who owned the Chinese carryout restaurant a few blocks from where Annette lived. She had never made a connection with the restaurant owner before, but this time Annette's radiant personality, and her loving and joyous presence, melted the woman's gruff demeanor. Over the next few weeks the two became good friends.

It was this restaurant owner, this synchronistic connection that had been made, who ended up alerting Annette to the prospect of buying a building a few doors away. It was underpriced but not yet on the real estate market. That building became what is now the Georgetown Healing Arts Center.

For more than half of Annette's life she has practiced and taught yoga and meditation classes. "I thank my lucky stars that I started those practices," Annette told me. "Meditation was like planting a seed and every day you water it with your daily practice, and one day when you need it, you realize there is a huge structure within that has developed to support you. The practices have cultivated my ability to hear the whispers of my intuitive voice."

Annette's thoughts on luck and life are spoken with an infectious enthusiasm, and from a "place in self" of rock-solid integrity. "I make my own luck. Luck is the power of attraction. I live like my heart is open. When you live with your heart open, the world opens its heart to you. Love is a verb. Love is action. When you give it to the clerk or the taxi driver, or anyone you meet in life, it is reflected back to you. The genesis of luck is love. Act more loving and you attract more good fortune.

"Everyone wants to be lucky. When you feel better about yourself you attract so much more of the positive. Most of my therapeutic practice is about my clients learning to live a full and fun life. Bad luck, if used properly, and if we draw the proper lessons from it, can be turned into an advantage. Luck can be whatever you need, rather than just what you want. Luck can be peace of mind. Luck is serendipity. It is being in touch with Spirit."

Lifelong Streaks of "Survivor" Luck

Some guys have all the luck, some guys have all the pain are the lyrics of a Rod Stewart song that came to mind as I pondered the story of Carl Chambers, a retired Dallas public school principal. I met him through my father at a coffee shop that both men frequent in rural East Texas. Chambers, 71 years old when I interviewed him, traces his luck back to the early 1950s, during the Korean War.

"My very first day in Korea as a sergeant draftee, a mortar round fell near me and a piece of metal put a big crease in my helmet. That became my lucky helmet and I wore it the entire war. Another time I was up in a tree with a bunch of other soldiers and I climbed down just before a round blew that tree and the soldiers in it apart. Three times altogether I should have been dead. It was like a guardian angel was sitting on my shoulder."

Chambers survived the war unscathed and returned to Texas, where his luck found expression in stock investments, games of chance, and the avoidance of health problems or injury in accidents. He fell off ladders and out of trees and from other heights at least ten times in his life and never broke a bone. He's been to Las Vegas a dozen times and won $500 or more playing nickel and quarter slot machines at least eleven of those twelve trips. He's been a bettor at racetracks, playing his hunches on the horses, betting his picks in those moments when "a feeling of confidence comes over me," and the result has been regular winnings. His luckiest streak of all came from his investments in the stock market. Over a twelve-year period, from 1988 to 2000, he turned $2,000 into a $1.2 million nest egg, and pulled most of that money out of the market just two months before the bubble burst and the collapse in values began.

"I've been lucky as hell all my life," Chambers marvels. "I can't explain it except in terms of a guardian angel. It's like I've been protected, and all I have to do is to count my blessings."

When it comes to having a lifelong streak of luck around the survival of life-threatening accidents, my father qualifies as inordinately lucky. His work in the oil drilling business as a roughneck, driller, toolpusher, and finally as the owner of an oil drilling company placed him continually in harm's way for more than forty years. Oil drilling has traditionally ranked with coal mining as one of the world's most hazardous and accident-prone types of work. My father's narrow escapes, like a proverbial cat with nine lives, underscores that danger.

At 20 years of age, while standing 90 feet up inside an oil derrick, his safety belt failed. He plummeted 12 feet before a knot at the end of a rope around his waist miraculously snagged on a metal beam and broke his fall, which would have otherwise resulted in certain death on the rig's iron floor below. Five years later, a 30-foot length of drilling pipe fell from a derrick onto his back and head, paralyzing him from the waist down. He was lucky to be alive, but doctors were even more amazed at his luck in recovering from the paralysis after several months—and returning to work. The same roughneck whose negligence caused this accident to my father was injured in a similar mishap several years later and paralyzed for life. Another time my father was the only person on the drilling rig floor when a malfunction released 12 tons of iron from the derrick, all of which fell in a thunderous roar all around him, coming to rest within inches but not inflicting a scratch.

Since retiring from the oil business my father has been a rancher, raising herds of black angus cattle. One stormy afternoon he was stepping out of his pickup truck to check on some cattle when a tremendous bolt of lightning struck at his feet, instantly killing five large cows and a bull, yet leaving him unscathed. He had one hand on the door handle, an instant from death. At the age of 76, he fell beneath his tractor and it kicked out of gear and ran over him. The huge rear wheel rolled over him and he lay there for a few minutes, marveling that he wasn't dead, before slowly getting up and brushing himself off. He had only been bruised.

It could be argued that my father is accident-prone and his good luck is really about overcoming instances of bad luck. Yet, no matter what your perspective, his dance with fate, or with a guardian angel, still ultimately adds up to the good fortune of staying alive. When I ask what he ascribes his luck to, he shakes his head in wonder. "I don't know. It's just one of those mysteries."

Some of the luckiest people I have encountered in my life are the least likely to publicly credit luck as a factor in their success or good fortune. Several multimillionaires I knew twenty years or more ago, before they became wealthy, declined to be interviewed for this book, citing reasons that sounded suspiciously superstitious. One, a man I'll call Paul, who retired rich in his forties, explained in a phone conversation, "If I talk about the role of luck I feel like I might jinx everything." In the background, I could hear Paul's knuckles knocking rapidly against the wood of his desk.

At a coffeehouse near my residence where I drink caffeine concoctions and read the newspaper most mornings, I met and became friends with a man who embodies a special form of "survivor" luck, and whose infectious, life-affirming humor and spirit have become an inspiration to others. Tom was 69 years old when we became acquainted. A native New Yorker from the Bronx, he's literally been a jack-of-all-trades throughout his life, holding a degree in electronics but having worked as a wilderness guide, bartender, bricklayer, fruit picker, and floor cleaner in a merchant ship's engine room.

Tom had been diagnosed at age 68 with an aggressive and rare form of bladder cancer that had spread to his prostate. Doctors gave him only a few months to live. This diagnosis came only a few months after he had recovered from open-heart surgery. Many people would have been overwhelmed by such a streak of bad luck. Tom admits he felt "the heaviness of death," yet he had the confidence of knowing that he had gracefully danced with danger and skillfully escaped from harm's way since childhood.

At least a dozen times, at various points in his life, Tom had gone to sleep not expecting to wake up again. Three of those instances had been suicide attempts with drug overdoses while in his twenties, a period in his life when he was bipolar and drinking heavily. Though too old to be drafted for Vietnam, Tom went to Southeast Asia at the height of the war nonetheless, as a civilian wandering around Cambodia and defying the risks just to see for himself what was happening.

"There's no way I could have survived or lived through some of my lifestyles without being somehow blessed," Tom told me.

While in his forties and living in northern California, Tom had been present as a close friend, Pete, slowly died of cancer. During the decline in his friend's health, Tom had been impressed and inspired by how beautifully an attending hospice nurse had handled the man's passing, and in turn how accepting of the death process his friend had become. After Pete's death, another of Tom's close friends, Johnny, was diagnosed with cancer, and Tom went through a similar death process with him, even dealing with the same hospitals and doctors. "My friends began to call me the Angel of Death," Tom says with his characteristic wry humor. "The joke became, don't get too friendly with Tom or you'll die."

Over the years Tom became a regular volunteer at hospices, contributing an irreverence about life and its foibles that kept cancer patients laughing until the end. Then came Tom's heart surgery, and following that, the most ironic twist of his life, a cancer diagnosis. He had surgery to remove the tumors, underwent radiation treatments, and did a regimen of holistic health treatments. But the more significant therapy for him was the treatment he gave his spirit.

"So I wouldn't die a piece at a time, the solution to me meant doing something creative. I built a creek, a pond, and a gazebo on my property. My attitude of survival was also about going into the witness position. I looked at my life and said, 'Boy, that was interesting. I wonder what that's all about.' They said I had less than a year to live, but a year after having said that, the three doctors who examined me couldn't find the cancer. It had disappeared."

In the jargon of medical science, when a recovery defies the odds, Tom was someone who "got real lucky." For his part, Tom isn't certain what luck means. "I have no idea what luck is for myself, or for anyone else. But I know luck isn't accidental. Luck is all a matter of perception. I am blessed by having a wonderful and supportive wife and daughter. They are my good fortune. Life is a spiritual journey, and the longer you stay alive and survive is not necessarily about luck. Sometimes it just means your work here hasn't been finished."

Embracing the Spiritual Nature of Reality

· Brian O'Mahony left Ireland and came to the United States in 1975, at the age of 25, with a degree in electrical engineering and a spiritual hunger. He became a devotee of a spiritual teacher, a former Lutheran minister named Franklin Jones, who had gone on a pilgrimage to India and returned with a new name and an inspirational message that blended elements from all of the world's major religions. In 1979, Brian and another devotee started an engineering consultant company, O'Mahony and Myer Electrical Engineering and Lighting Design, in the San Francisco Bay Area. Neither had taken a business management course or read a how-to business book.

"We established our business on the fundamental principle of giving as the key to good fortune. While we pay ourselves and our employees well, we also donate company profits at the end of each year. We have found firsthand that giving of yourself and of your resources is essential to attracting luck. Luck is created. You invest in it, and then it's a force that you can attract."

Spiritual considerations are never removed from business decisions in this company. Brian gives one of many examples. "Whenever I do a fee proposal for major projects, I always round off to an auspicious number like 108, which is auspicious in many spiritual traditions. All of our fee proposals that we've done for successful projects are multiples of 108, and I truly believe there is something about the use of that number which has affected our ability to get contracts." During the 1980s and 1990s, as the company grew to twenty-six employees and revenues increased an average of ten percent a year, numerous civic centers, libraries, and other high-profile projects were completed, including the Four Seasons Hotel Tower and the Sony Entertainment Center in San Francisco, the Saudi Arabian Customs Building, and the lighting for an entire new city in the Philippines.

In his personal life Brian sees his luck mirroring the good fortune of his company. He frequently wins large raffles, collecting a Rolex watch in one and a hi-fi system in another. "I knew I was going to win," he told me. "I felt lucky and connected to this invisible force, as if the stars had lined up. It's a feeling of certainty and confidence that comes over me. We always had this feeling about the company. We knew that it would succeed if we founded it on the premise that the wealth of the business was going to serve something honorable. We never entertained the possibility that the business would fail."

This confidence and certainty and faith is part of what separates lucky people from unlucky people. "Lucky people have an innate certainty that things will turn out with good fortune. Unlucky people still have doubt. My wife and I knew a woman who was unlucky. She kept starting these businesses and enterprises with great energy and fanfare, and they would always fail. She had a fundamental certainty that she would fail. She also had a need to fail. She had been abused as a child and there was something in her that needed every story to have a sad ending. Sometimes you have to dig deep to find out why you are unlucky."

One of Brian's spiritual practices—another key, he believes, to his success in attracting luck—is the use of a prayer that his spiritual teacher calls the Prayer of Changes. "We pray for good things to happen. But it's not a prayer to God for material things. That doesn't work. Instead, it's a prayer to release everything in you which presumes a limitation, or creates negative assumptions. You breathe that out, and you breathe in the vision of what you hope to achieve, and then you act on that with faith and confidence. You begin to see things shift around in your life. It creates a process where luck can occur."

Brian's friend Carol Otness, a 50-year-old preschool teacher, successfully used the prayer during three gambling trips to play slot machines in Reno, Nevada. On her first foray in April 1998, to celebrate her mother's birthday, she felt open to the possibility of winning, yet felt no attachment to the outcome, largely because she had never been a gambler. She experienced an immediate case of beginner's luck, winning exactly $108 worth of quarters, a number she interpreted as a "very auspicious" synchronicity.

After cashing in her winnings she decided to try one more quarter slot machine before leaving the casino with her mother and cousins. Fortune smiled again. She hit a $1,200 jackpot. "I jumped up and down, shouting yahoo and making a real scene." Afterwards, she meditated for an hour, giving thanks for this blessing.

The next year, once again in April, Carol went back to the Reno area, this time to Lake Tahoe with her husband Alex to celebrate their twentieth wedding anniversary. They stayed at Caesar's Palace, where Carol had an intuitive hint that she should play on a particular bank of quarter machines while sitting next to her husband. "I felt in a zone, so happy, just putting in three quarters at a time," Carol told me. " I started winning $30, then $60, and all of a sudden I hit three sevens and won a $1,000 jackpot."

After collecting her winnings, Carol sensibly stopped playing because intuitively she knew this was all she could expect to win on this trip. "I always stopped playing when I felt the moment had changed and realized that I had gotten disconnected from the flow. I would feel it in my body and just know that I wasn't attuned to a spirit current anymore. When I'm in that winning space it feels electrical to me, like I've opened to conductivity. I feel a resonance with the machine when I am winning."

Her third and final trip to play slots came in April 2001, when she made a trip by herself to Lake Tahoe. This time she was experimenting with a variety of signs and portents to supplement her usual spiritual tools. "An astrologer had given me the days in April where I would be lucky. April 25 was one of those days, so that's the one I chose to play on. I did the Prayer of Changes on the drive to Tahoe. I also used feng shui once I got there. I went to several casinos to find which machines were pointed due south, which is my fortune direction."

"At midnight I went to the machines I had chosen earlier inside Caesar's Palace. I played three quarter machines simultaneously. Within half an hour I had won $1,500 on those machines. I stopped playing at that point just as soon as I felt in my body that I had disconnected at the heart. The next day I drove home with my $1,500. I don't have any urge to go back. It's like those three trips and the three jackpots were openings for me, showing how I can align myself with the blessings of good fortune. Now my practice is to keep myself aligned with spirit."

A former Michigan symphony orchestra clarinetist, Bill Somers, received the nickname "Lucky" after his spiritual teacher sent him on a two-week blackjack junket to Las Vegas in 1998. The length and intensity of his playing time, the rapid ebb and flow of his luck, and the unusual spiritual mission motivating him to play should earn him a place of distinction in the Gambling Hall of Fame.

Somers was a skillful blackjack player who used his own system of counting cards, but attributed most of his success to channeling periodic streaks of luck. On several occasions he played for four hours at a stretch in Las Vegas casinos and won $7,000 or more. "When I was on a win streak, it would feel like a force had descended over the table that was beneficial to me. It gave me utter confidence in my luck. Once I played for eight hours at Treasure Island in Vegas and it felt like the force had descended. It felt like I couldn't be defeated. I won $10,000 and then had a losing streak down to $2,000. But I knew my luck would come back. I was sitting there at the table, laughing, I was so certain my luck would return. It did, and I got back to $6,500 in winnings and quit."

In early 1998, Somers's spiritual teacher asked him to undertake a blackjack-playing junket to Las Vegas as a spiritual experiment. For up to fourteen hours a day, every day for more than two weeks, at five Las Vegas casinos, Somers played blackjack as if his life depended on it. "Every hour of every day I sat there at those blackjack tables, just facing the feeling that winning was good, and losing was bad. In the midst of all this I was engaged in spiritual practices and invoking my spiritual teacher."

Halfway through this experiment, Somers had accumulated winnings of $20,000, and he seemed to win no matter where he played. At one point he was dealt fourteen winning hands in a row. Then his luck turned sour quickly and dramatically. For the final week, no matter what strategy he used, no matter which casino he played in, he couldn't seem to win. When he had broken even again, after hundreds of thousands of hands of blackjack, he and his spiritual teacher agreed to end the experiment.

Afterwards, his spiritual teacher told him: "You've got the gambler's mentality about life. When you're winning, everything seems great. But when you're losing, everything about your whole life seems in jeopardy."

The lesson that Somers drew from this experience was life-altering. "I realized that the gambler mentality is an addict mentality about life. How I played blackjack was how I lived my life. And all of luck is really just a play on the spiritual world. I have since stopped gambling altogether and devoted myself to leading a spiritual life."

Intuition and Luck: The Link to Spirituality

Possibly the best and simplest analogy I have ever encountered for spiritual transcendence comes from a physicist, Michio Kaku. Imagine that we humans are like a family of goldfish living in a bowl of water. We have accepted our world and our life as it appears. Then one day, a fish from among us leaps too high and flops out of the bowl, lying out there until something (a cosmic hand) picks it up and places it back inside.

During those moments the fish was outside the bowl it was able to see all of us fellow fish inside it, and a realization dawned that "this is where I come from." On its return, the fish attempts to inform us of a world outside our own, beyond our bowl, and the fish is met with disbelief and maybe ridicule. Was that venturesome fish lucky to have had a transcendent experience?

Those synchronicities, intuitive hunches, premonitions, precognitive dreams, and other extrasensory experiences we have examined in this book, along with spiritual and mystical moments, periodically jolt some of us outside the "bowl" of our consensus-reality perceptions.

Dr. Judith Orloff considers a person's psychic attunement to be an extension of his or her connection to spirit. "Even though people can improve their intuition without a spiritual reference point, the power that comes from this can be seductive, and their egos often get out of control."

Sir Alister Hardy, while director of religious experience research at Oxford University, also drew a link between the psychic and spiritual realms. "The influence which religious people feel when they say they are in touch with what seems to them to be some transcendental element—a power that affects their lives, whether they call if God or not—may be something within the same field as extrasensory telepathic communication." Perhaps, Sir Hardy continues, the element at the heart of all religion is "some extrasensory shared spiritual experience . . . tapped by those who may have discovered or learnt the way of making rapport with it—something perhaps like the collective unconscious of Jung?"

There is a range of tools and practices available to you, each designed to access your intuition and to reach beyond into the spiritual realm. Judee Gee, the Australian director of The Intuition School in France, and author of the book *Intuition*, calls the I Ching and the tarot cards "symbolic tools of divination" that can help to "diminish the human tendency to engage in self-deception and self-delusion in the interpretation of intuitive information." These intermediary methods, relying strongly on intuitive capacity, help us to avoid "the potential traps of power, manipulation, and illusion that are always present when we utilize our intuition."

Practices such as regular prayer and meditation help to create inner structures through which we can channel our intuitive capacities. Neuroscientist and physician Mona Lisa Schulz offers this perspective on the value of that process: "Divine consciousness speaks to your human consciousness, offering us quick, keen insights into the problems of everyday life and suggesting potential solutions through the language of intuition—the language of the soul."

The Power of Prayer

Most of us seem to resort to prayer only when we desire something, or to relieve pain and suffering when we feel there is no other healthy recourse through which to channel our desperation. By treating the process of prayer in this manner, we may be neglecting the powerful advantage that it bestows on those who use it with regular, ritualized intention.

Prayer aligns human will with divine will. It is in the realm of healing that we find the powers of prayer gaining the most scientific validity. Some experiments in long-distance healing and prayer have revealed extraordinary effects. For a working definition of distance healing, let's use the one I found in some of the medical literature: "a conscious, dedicated act of mentation attempting to benefit another person's physical or emotional well-being at a distance." This process is called "intercessory" prayer.

The most well-publicized studies occurred at San Francisco General Hospital and the Kansas City Mid-America Heart Institute, both of which found that prayed-for patients healed faster and more completely than patients not receiving prayers. In these and other similar studies, half of the patients were randomly assigned to a group that received no prayer intervention, while the other half were assigned to a group in which people they didn't know prayed for their recovery. Heart patients at the San Francisco facility required less assistance breathing, and needed fewer antibiotics and diuretics than patients assigned to a control group who didn't receive prayer attention.

A study that appeared in a June 2000 edition of the *Annals of Internal Medicine,* written by medical researchers at the University of Maryland, used a "meta-analysis" on twenty-three clinical trials of prayer that involved more than 2,700 patients, and found that distinct positive effects on health had been documented. "Absolutely, the evidence suggests that something may be going on," declared the lead study author, Dr. John Astin. "I'm open-minded to possibilities of things we don't understand."

Prayer studies in general have concluded that the prayers were more effective when the praying person asked merely for God's presence rather than asking for a specific result. Prayer also seems to work no matter what your belief system—Christian, Jewish, Buddhist, whatever. Psychiatrist Judith Orloff contends that it doesn't even matter whether you appeal in your prayer to a force outside yourself or to an inner wisdom. "While meditation is an open-ended way of listening to spirit, prayer is a specific way of speaking to it." While this seems to be true, there is also evidence that, at least in one respect, not all spiritual beliefs are equally beneficial. "People with positive spiritual beliefs—such as the idea that God represents love and forgiveness—do better than those who believe in harsh divine punishment," observes Dr. Marty Sullivan, an associate professor of medicine at Duke University School of Medicine.

Responding to the criticism that prayer has a placebo effect and works only because a person thinks it will (which to my mind is in and of itself a remarkable power), Dr. Sullivan counters that in most of the prayer studies the patients didn't know they were being prayed for, nor did their doctors know. Dr. Sullivan has also seen other studies in which "prayer can even affect the growth of yeast and other laboratory organisms. Obviously, these are not affected by the power of positive thinking."

Are the really lucky people the ones who have mastered the art of prayer? Is their relationship to spirit opened in a particular way that enables good fortune to flow more readily? Can group prayer directed at individuals, much like the experiments in distance healing, work in the realm of luck and reversing bad fortune? Is the "energy force," whatever it is, utilized in distance healing the same channel through which premonitions and other psi effects occur? These and related questions, though they remain largely unanswered, do suggest future paths for research.

Meditation

Quieting the mind using a meditation practice can enable us to listen more effectively to our intuitive voice. Physiologically, meditative practices have been shown to lower blood pressure, slow the metabolism, and relieve stress—reason enough for some people to undertake the regimen.

Based on my own experience and observation in twelve-day consciousness workshops, combining daily meditation with group dreamwork, silence and fasting, art, music, and other techniques enables us to shift gradually into a more intuitive state of mind that facilitates our ability to discern patterns. These patterns, internal and external, sensing the ebb and flow of events and energetic trends, clue us intuitively into taking actions that can give us the appearance of having gotten lucky.

"The secret of meditation lies somewhere between the effort of trying and the ease of letting go," says former Buddhist monk Donald Altman in his book, *Living Kindness*. "In this sense it resembles sports, where you have to be at your best, alert and in the zone, but totally relaxed and calm at the same time."

"By meditating," continues Altman, "you will increase the strength of your mind to do almost any activity. . . . It also means you will be better able to focus your mind on breaking habits or loosening the grip of harmful choices and patterns . . . (and) meditative practice can generate synchronicities."

A technology called magneto-encephalography has been used on meditators to measure their brain activity before, during, and after meditation. Brain waves at several frequencies were found to be occurring during meditation, including at 40Hz oscillations. That particular frequency corresponds to what some neuroscientists have described as "the most likely neural basis for consciousness itself." In other words, the act of meditation seems to tap into the most direct source of our fundamental awareness as conscious beings.

Mantras, Affirmations, Yoga

Reciting mantras is a mind focus practice that involves one or more sacred words. Mantras are most common in the Buddhist and Hindu traditions, and date back to at least 1500 B.C., but most spiritual belief systems use a variation of them. A Christian contemplative version is known as "The Jesus Prayer," in which the user repeats over and over a phrase about Jesus and mercy. The repetition of sacred words, says Donald Altman, is "a doorway through which the presence of God or self-knowing can enter. . . . Mantras possess vibrational energy that moves through all levels of physical and spiritual being. Like a transmitter, repetition increases the strength and reach of a mantra's signal."

In similar fashion, affirmations, which usually don't contain sacred or spiritual words, help us to express clearly what we want, to set an intention, and to condition ourselves to believe that we are deserving. By making an affirmation repetitively over time, we reprogram our unconscious minds, creating a vibrational resonance with our goal, much as what happens using the laws of attraction. "Affirmations are positive statements you make to yourself which consciously program the unconscious part of your mind and set the stage for self-fulfilling prophecy," write Charlene Belitz and Meg Lundstrom in their book, *The Power of Flow*.

Yoga is another mind-quieting practice that has been shown to help asthma sufferers, improve cardiovascular health, relieve chronic back pain, and provide help for some mental health problems, such as obsessive-compulsive disorders. Despite the emphasis in Western culture on yoga as physical movement and stretching, yoga has its roots in meditation, and Eastern cultures have traditionally engaged it first and foremost as a gateway, a mind-body connective route, to higher states of consciousness.

No matter which mind-quieting practice you undertake—meditation, mantras, yoga—you should be careful about directly infusing the practice with an intention or goal that involves the direct enhancement of your material well-being. Meditation and yoga weren't designed to facilitate anything other than spiritual development. Mantras, however, much like the positive thinking of affirmations and visualizations, do carve out a clearer role for willful intentions.

Once again I refer to Altman: "A wish or a dream for something like winning the lottery may only be another kind of craving and attachment. When you create an intention, take care that it is direct, honest, and clear. While there are mantras for almost everything from finding a loving relationship and healing to creating abundance, what manifests also depends on your subconscious thoughts. Consciously, you might want a relationship, but if you subconsciously feel undeserving, then the mantra will not bring satisfactory results."

The I Ching and the Tarot
Each system among these tools of divination, by tapping directly into intuition, may release a person's natural psi abilities. The I Ching is a system for using chance to seek advice, the earliest known such system. You formulate a question and go through a ritual of either separating yarrow sticks or tossing coins. This process randomly picks one of 64 hexagrams, each of which consists of six lines corresponding to a passage of explanation linked to a hexagram in the accompanying book. The underlying idea is that chance provides a way through the I Ching for seekers to tap into the flow of the universe.

In *Netherworld*, his book about ancient man's attempts to know the future, Orientalist scholar Robert K. G. Temple calls the I Ching an attempt "to reduce a means of consulting fate to a system" based on a "profound Chinese tradition of the nature of time, space, and the universe." This system "shows a striking correspondence with the mathematical system of binary arithmetic, which has become the basis for the operation of modern computers." Temple is the first Westerner I know of to find a connection between the I Ching and early forms of the game of chess, which is played on a board with 64 squares corresponding to the 64 hexagrams of the I Ching. Chess originated in China, not in India as is commonly believed, and some ancient Chinese chess pieces have been found inscribed with symbols from the I Ching.

"Like all good oracles, I Ching passages are worded with great metaphysical generality," writes statistician Mike Orkin in *What Are the Odds?*, "so in some sense the I Ching can never be wrong. One might suggest that such generality makes the I Ching meaningless; however, any information that gives the seeker new insights could hardly be called meaningless." A 1971 experiment in New York conducted by Charles Honorton and Lawrence Rubin found that subjects who were believers in psi got answers from the I Ching relevant to their questions at a level significantly higher than people who were skeptical of psi.

Tarot cards are western civilization's parallel system of divination to the I Ching. Originally designed as playing cards, the first well-documented decks were produced in France in the fourteenth century, commissioned by Charles VI, though some historians believe the concept of such a deck originated much earlier in Egypt. Today's decks consist of seventy-eight cards, each illustrated with colorful figures of a medieval design, and each symbolizing primary forces of both the material and spiritual worlds. The Wheel of Fortune card, for instance, symbolizes a person's fate. Dr. Mona Lisa Schulz calls the cards "a helpful imagery channel" for focusing attention in our lives. The cards "are the jumper cables" for our intuitive engines.

Feng Shui

Derived from the I Ching, this ancient Chinese philosophy of attracting health and prosperity is based on organizing a person's living or working space to align with the movement of "qi" energies. Feng shui is the art of placement—of everyday objects, rooms, plants—to promote balance and harmony. For instance, to increase prosperity you might hang a mirror on the wall behind the stove in your kitchen, creating a reflection of the stove burners that has a symbolic effect of intensifying the fires of prosperity. There is a prosperity corner in every house, usually best identified by a feng shui consultant, as well as a relationship corner, and each requires special attention to the placement of beds, doorways, mirrors, and other aspects of living space.

A novel take on feng shui, relating it to the inner structure of our mind and our thoughts, comes from Lillian Too and her book, *Inner Feng Shui*. She describes how we can make ourselves "feel lucky by thinking of all the good things that happen in life. All the opportunities that came your way, all the big breaks you got. All the accidents you missed. All the good health you enjoy. You are lucky even to be alive.... Thinking lucky thoughts brings you good luck, thinking unlucky thoughts brings you bad luck. It is as simple as that!"

Astrology

Perhaps the oldest and most widely practiced form of divination, astrology has been a source of fascination for many personages who qualify as lucky people. Among the personalities seeking guidance from it have been President Grover Cleveland; financier J. Pierpont Morgan, who had a personal astrologer to advise him on all of his financial decisions and who once made the statement that "Millionaires don't use astrology, billionaires do"; New York Stock Exchange Presidents Jacob Stout and Seymour Cromwell; Richard Jenrette, a founder of the securities firm, Donaldson, Lufkin, and Jenrette; and, in more recent times, First Lady Nancy Reagan and President Ronald Reagan.

Its origins date back to the ancient Chaldeans and Babylonians of Mesopotamia, whose priests blended astronomy and astrology as one science of interactions between Heaven and Earth. A band of stars across the night horizon was divided into twelve houses, each representing some important aspect of life. In turn, the earth's orbital plane is divided into twelve equal sections of thirty degrees. Each of the twelve signs of the zodiac bears the name of a constellation, such as Gemini and Pisces. These signs are said to affect every human being's destiny, as calculated by their birthdate, time of birth, and the latitude and longitude of the place of birth.

Numerology

Some people regard certain numbers as either lucky or unlucky for them. An accountant named William Barber used a stock market prediction system based on numerology to make himself a wealthy man. As described in Max Gunther's book, *The Luck Factor*, in numerology "there is a mysterious connecting link between numbers and the events in human life. If the numbers are lucky, the events will supposedly be lucky." Barber's odd method involved taking the results of several annual sporting events, such as the college Rose Bowl game, and applying them to the stock market, forecasting whether it would end up or down at the end of each year. Gunther confirmed that Barber's system had worked for him every year he had tried it from 1964 to 1975. There is some evidence to suggest, however, that numerology isn't a predictive mechanism, but simply creates a structure onto which we project our unconscious to elicit intuition's ability to find meaning. Sometimes the law of averages alone will prove us right.

The Laws of Karma

Have you ever known someone who seemed destined to have good luck, as if he were acting out a sort of life plan that had been scripted the day he was born? Or maybe you have felt as if you were on a track headed in one bad-luck direction and were powerless to get off. This may be where the phrases "good karma" and "bad karma" come into play. Karma is the moral law of cause and effect in our thoughts and actions, comparable to the Biblical statement, "Whatsoever a man soweth, that shall he also reap" (Gal. 6:7). Under karmic laws, we repeat mistakes until they are corrected, if not in this lifetime then in a future lifetime, which leads us to the concept of reincarnation.

At one time in their formative stages, Judaism, Christianity, and Islam all embraced reincarnation, the transmigration of souls, as part of their religious philosophy. Hinduism and Buddhism still accept the idea. In the case of Christianity, the belief in reincarnation was expunged from the faith and the Bible in 553 A.D., during the fifth Ecumenical Council of Constantinople, at the behest of the Emperor Justinian.

A late-nineteenth century Hindu mystic, Swami Vivekananda, likened karma and reincarnation to a chain with black links alternating with white links, an endless repetition of these links, in which by knowing the nature of one link you know the chain. "Likewise, all our lives—past, present, and future—form, as it were, an infinite chain, without beginning and without end, each unit of which is one life, with two ends: birth and death. What we are and what we do here in this life is being repeated again and again . . . so we see that our present life in this world has been exactly determined by our previous lives, that is to say, by our own past actions. Just as we go out of this world with the sum total of our present actions upon us, so we come into it with the sum total of our past actions upon us."

A Buddhist perspective on karma has been summarized by the Tibetan monk, Sogyal Rinpoche, in his classic work, *The Tibetan Book of Living and Dying*. "The word "karma" literally means 'action,' and karma is both the power latent within actions, and the results our actions bring. It means that whatever we do, with our body, speech, or mind, will have a corresponding result. Each action, even the smallest, is pregnant with its consequences. . . . The results of our action are often delayed, even into future lifetimes; we cannot pin down one cause, because any event can be an extremely complicated mixture of many karmas ripening together. So we tend to assume now that things happen to us 'by chance,' and when everything goes well, we simply call it 'good luck.' "

Secrets of Spiritual Luck

What sets lucky people who are spiritual apart from other lucky people who are oblivious to spiritual matters? Though I'm not aware of studies in this regard, it certainly seems reasonable to assume that atheists and people lacking spiritual guidance do experience good fortune. Atheists have probably won the lottery. Agnostics probably do find long-term happiness in relationships. But nearly all of the people I interviewed for this book, and many of the truly fortunate people I have observed in my life, appear to attract luck, at least in part, because they interpret seemingly random events as guided and meaningful, rather than as a byproduct of a chaotic and spiritless existence.

Scientific ultra-rationalist atheists believe that our brains—and the entire universe, for that matter—amount to nothing more than machines that evolved to be complex solely as the result of chance. Inventor Arthur Young, in his book *The Reflexive Universe*, answered by noting that "there never was a machine that did not have a purpose." Psychologist Stan Gooch adds, "Chance cannot by itself produce anything meaningful." Chance might provide the chemistry in nature to produce natural glass, for instance, but chance will never create a wine bottle!

Most people blessed with good fortune believe that design played a role in its acquisition, and they sense how each life fits into a larger mosaic.

To them good fortune isn't just about the extent of material abundance—it's about how many blessings we can count in all aspects of our lives. They also understand that good luck isn't always a literal response to what we want; usually it is a blessing bestowed to satisfy what we most need.

Attracting luck into our lives often involves consciously embracing faith.

As William Arthur Ward once wrote, "Faith is knowing there is an ocean because you have seen a brook." For many of us that "brook" is correctly interpreting a synchronicity, or an intuitive insight, or a precognitive dream, and following these signposts until good fortune manifests into our reality.

Lucky people respect the luck-attraction powers their own generosity can set in motion.

President Abraham Lincoln's career in politics, for instance, was launched by a synchronicity that occurred because of his generous nature. A destitute stranger had approached Lincoln in Illinois and asked the young woodcutter to buy a barrel of discarded junk for a dollar. The man needed the money so he could eat. Solely out of kindness, Lincoln bought the barrel and days passed before he finally cleaned it out. Inside he found law books, Blackstone's *Commentaries,* in an almost complete edition. The chance acquisition of these books inspired Lincoln to pursue his career as a lawyer, a profession that enabled him to obtain the knowledge and contacts for election to the U.S. Congress and later to the presidency.

Lucky people understand that good luck is sabotaged by greed.

An out-of-control ego generates greed, and greed short-circuits the luck-making process with impulsive and compulsive behaviors that flip good luck into bad. Envy can have the same effect by making us feel like failures in comparison to others. Spiritual practices help us to tame unruly egos.

Lucky people attract their own luck by the way they think about life as a victor, never the victim.

That's what a professional prosperity coach, Darel Rutherford, author of *Being the Solution,* told me when I asked about the connections he saw between luck, our thoughts, and spirituality. "As human beings, two spiritual laws govern us. We become what we think about, and what we have in life must correspond exactly to who we are *being*. According to those spiritual laws, the pattern of your thinking decides who you will *be*. And your choice of *being* determines what belongs in your life. You have the power to create your own reality, and the power to choose whom you will *be* in that reality."

As we have seen in the stories of lucky people animating this book, one essential ingredient for leading a fortunate life is an optimistic attitude. To build that positive outlook we must be mindful of our actions and our impact on others, express our gratitude for what we treasure, be generous in spirit, and avoid toxic people and toxic thoughts. Taken together, all of the luck secrets described in the previous pages are about the art and mastery of living life to its fullest. Happiness is a moment-to-moment choice. True fortune is a mystery of the heart.

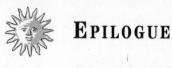

EPILOGUE

Lucky Me!

My journey tracking Lady Luck's shadow began at a time when I was thrashing about, lost in the wilderness of adversity and despair, feeling as if the upheavals in my life signaled an abandonment by good fortune. That dark night of the soul not only receded in a rapid and dramatic fashion, its replacement by a wellspring of hope and prosperity propelled me into ever deeper considerations, resulting in this book. For that, I feel humbly blessed, exceedingly lucky, and eternally grateful.

As I reflect on the personal lessons learned at the various stages of my exploration—from the misfortune that morphed into a run of good fortune, then into this book's research phase, when I began to discover the secrets of lucky people—it seems clear that the beginning of my own lucky streak also marked, not coincidentally, my initiation into a process of releasing attachment to outcomes. It wasn't that I no longer cared about my fate and future. Quite the contrary. But I had surrendered to a higher power and released my need to feel in control. That surrender now enables me to experience serendipity without judgment, to respond to its appearance in my life as a meaningful guidepost, and to trust in my intuition as a clear channel to the divine.

At least once in each of our lives, a doorway briefly opens, giving us access to another realm, a glimpse at another way of being. You may recall how, in the movie *Lost Horizon,* a group of Western explorers found the fabled but hidden city of peace and contentment when a break in the inclement weather revealed a passage through the snow-clogged mountains. Even after these Westerners experienced the magic of Shangri-la, they felt compelled to leave in response to the distractions of their outer lives. Once they deserted paradise, they spent the rest of their days searching for a way back in again. So it is with the flow of luck. Once its mysterious portal opens to us, once we have channeled its energy with sustained intensity, we yearn for its return, and we are never quite the same again.

My experience with the magic of luck changed me irrevocably. It matured my perception of how the mind can shatter the illusion of limitations. It convinced me that luck truly is "an inside job," and each of us has a capacity to access it. More importantly, I realize how the opportunity that was presented for me to share what I've learned wasn't simply happenstance. This book constitutes my most gratifying stroke of good fortune. May it inspire and guide you in discovering the role of luck in your own life . . . and may fortune smile on your journey!

More Secrets of Lucky People

If you're a lucky person with secrets of luck to share about games of chance, business and investments, health, safety, or relationships, or if you have stories involving your dreams, intuitions, synchronicities, or precognitions, you are encouraged to contact the author through Kensington Publishing, 850 Third Avenue, New York, New York, 10022, or via the internet at rftruman@earthlink.net.

Author's Note: The following Appendixes elaborate on ideas or questions raised in Part Two, The Reach of the Mind. This material may help you to create a context for explaining how our minds can create a "luck" frequency of thoughts with a possible impact on the physical realms of reality.

 APPENDIX A

Theories to Explain Precognition

To illustrate the nature of the problem facing parapsychologists in detecting the energetic force, whatever it is, linking cause and effect in precognition, consider the problem facing researchers in another realm of science. By the year 2003, physicists still had not found direct evidence of gravity waves, the existence of which has been one of the fundamental predictions of Einstein's general theory of relativity for nearly a century. We know gravity exists because we feel its effects. Yet, while scientists are able to theorize about the mechanism that causes us to experience gravity, the act of measuring gravity "waves," the presumed cause of the effect, has proven to be a huge challenge. To measure gravity waves from another star, for instance, would require detecting an effect on Earth so weak that when waves reach us our entire planet momentarily expands and then contracts *the width of an atom* in response.

Parapsychologists do have theories, plenty of them, to explain the psi phenomena they detect. After observing precognition at work in his laboratory at UCLA's Neuropsychiatric Institute in Los Angeles, Dr. Barry Taff theorized that sometimes we "see" or sense the future by absorbing a "particle" from the space-time continuum, and this particle acts in accordance with holographic universe principles. Just as a holographic image has all the information about itself spread equally throughout it so that any one part can tell us about the whole, so might a "particle" of information, flowing without time constraints, connect us through sporadic glimpses into a larger body of information from our future.

(This particle idea reminds me of what some scientists have noted in relation to molecules of oxygen in the atmosphere. Since these molecules are recycled, the odds are high that each of us has breathed into our lungs at least one molecule that was formerly in the lungs of Julius Caesar or Jesus Christ 2,000 years ago.)

Nobel Prize–winning physicist Werner Heisenberg once described the level of reality we call quantum physics in terms that could be applied to human consciousness and psi: "When we get down to the atomic level, the objective world in space and time no longer exists, and the mathematical symbols of theoretical physics refer merely to possibilities, not to fact."

Proponents of consciousness physics suspect that the human mind, and the act of perception, can influence reality in concrete and measurable ways. "Experimental evidence increasingly suggests the observer and the observed are tied together," says physicist Menas Kafatos of George Mason University in Virginia. If true, human beings really can create their own luck or envision a new reality, to some extent, by affecting a critical threshold of matter at the subatomic level, willing trillions of atoms to interact and align in an advantageous way.

Under a model known as Decision Augmentation Theory, some parapsychological researchers argue that human success at influencing results produced by random number generators comes because some people can sense a favorable run of numbers and initiate their "Play" button pushes at the most advantageous moments. In that regard, people successful in these experiments are "statistical opportunists" at sensing and capturing "deviance" from otherwise truly random sequences of numbers.

High geomagnetic field activity caused by the solar wind, as we learned in Part Two, seems to diminish psi abilities. Either the geomagnetic fluctuations interfere with the mechanism of human physiology that detects psi stimuli, or somehow the psi signal is lost in the active geomagnetic field.

Another factor seeming to affect psi receptivity is "star time." Physicist James Spottiswoode of the Cognitive Sciences Laboratory in Palo Alto, California, reported in 1997 that from 1,468 published psi experiments, "whatever the effect being measured was more than tripled when the local sidereal time was near 13:30 (about 1:30)." Sidereal time is star time, expressed in relation to the earth's rotation and fixed stars overhead, and takes 23 hours and 56 minutes for one complete rotation.

To test this sidereal time finding further, Spottiswoode added another 1,015 trials from other psi experiments, and the anomalous cognition, as he calls psi, increased to become more than four times effective within one hour of 13:30 LST than at any other time of day or night. An implication of these findings, says Spottiswoode, "is that some property of the earth is important to anomalous cognition functioning." Earth could be acting either as an absorber of psi signals, or as a reflector.

APPENDIX B

Why Precognition May Not Always Be Replicable

"One of the fundamental requirements in the exact sciences is that an experiment should be repeatable and its outcome predictable," wrote Arthur Koestler in *The Roots of Coincidence*. "But it is in the very nature of parapsychological phenomena that they are not repeatable at will, and that they operate unpredictably."

University of California at Davis statistician Jessica Utts has done numerous statistical analyses of psi experimental data over the years, and writing in a 1996 edition of the *Journal of Scientific Exploration*, made a reasonable case that replicability in psi experiments is not as important as in other fields of science. "Few human capabilities are perfectly replicable on demand. For example, even the best hitters in the major baseball leagues cannot hit on demand. Nor can we predict when someone will hit or when they will score a home run. In fact, we cannot even predict whether or not a home run will occur in a particular game. That does not mean that home runs don't exist. . . . The same should be true of psychic functioning. Even if there truly is an effect, it may never be replicable on demand in the short run even if we understand how it works."

Scientists seem to debate endlessly the question of why experiments successfully demonstrating precognition and other luck-generating abilities are so difficult to repeat in the laboratory. Psi believers say this natural human capacity is simply too weak and erratic for science to extract it consistently from laboratory test subjects, a failing that in no way should invalidate the positive findings accumulated by thousands of experiments over the years. Psi skeptics reply that the failure to replicate these abilities consistently at will indicates that chance and coincidence alone account for any positive experimental results.

A possible path to resolution of this conflict may be found in the realm of quantum mechanics and experimental research into the subatomic level of reality. According to most theoretical physicists, the very act of scientists observing interactions at the subatomic level changes outcomes and influences the most fundamental forms of energy at the heart of matter. The magazine *Discover* (June 2002) posed the quandary in simple terms worth quoting here: "The boundary between an objective 'world out there' and our own subjective consciousness that seemed so clearly defined in physics before the eerie discoveries of the twentieth century blurs in quantum mechanics. When physicists look at the basic constituents of reality—atoms and their innards, or the particles of light called photons—what they see depends on how they have set up their experiment. A physicist's observations determine whether an atom, say, behaves like a fluid wave or a hard particle, or which path it follows in traveling from one point to another."

One of the most renowned physicists of the twentieth century, John Archibald Wheeler of Princeton University, believes that our act of observing subatomic interactions in the present can actually affect how certain particles, such as photons of light, behaved in the past. What he proposes is literally a form of precognition involving human consciousness, in the form of scientific observers, and energy in the form of the photons. An experiment in 1984 at the University of Maryland actually demonstrated this effect, showing that until the physicists had taken their measurements of a photon's trajectory, the photon's path had not yet been fixed. That's a real mind bender (or maybe photon bender), an affront to common sense, yet so are the examples of psi phenomena we have seen documented.

If the relationship between observers and the outcomes of experiments on quantum systems is interactive, if not symbiotic, why can't a similar phenomenon be happening in laboratories that attempt to measure that output of human consciousness we call psi? I am certainly not the first to note how the psi experiments of skeptics usually always turn out negative, while those conducted by psi investigators (or the open-minded) frequently turn up positive. This difference is not simply due to a difference in experimental safeguards. The actual state of mind itself seems to play an important role in the outcome of psi experiments. Knowing this, anyone can tap into psi simply by being open to its possibility.

APPENDIX C

A Paranormal Part of the Brain

Belief itself, when it comes to "psychic" abilities as well as mysticism, spirituality, religion, and God, seems to be hardwired into our brains. More specifically, hardwired into the right temporal lobes of our brains. In the 1990s, American and Canadian neuroscientists uncovered persuasive evidence that parts of the brain's temporal lobe, an area they named the "God module," is structured to produce feelings and effects of spiritual or mystical transcendence.

High-tech imaging techniques were used to map and observe this brain area when test subjects thought about religion or God. That area became much more electrically active during mystical thoughts. Similarly, when researchers applied electromagnetic pulsed stimulation to that part of the brain, test subjects experienced a variety of "paranormal" and other powerful psychological effects. One of the researchers, Professor Michael Persinger of Canada's Laurentian University, believes that natural fluctuations in the Earth's magnetic field may also periodically be stimulating this part of the human brain, reinforcing religious and mystical beliefs in people with more developed temporal lobes.

This discovery, commented Dr. John Gillies of the University of Glasgow's department of psychology, "does seem to suggest that the skeptic and the believer, the atheist and the devout, may be, in some sense, 'programmed' to hold the views that they do."

Other laboratory studies have produced evidence that meditation practices may stimulate the temporal lobe in a manner similar to the electromagnetic pulses. Veteran meditators were found to exhibit a greater number of paranormal-type experiences than people who had never meditated.

Dr. Melvin Morse, author of *Where God Lives*, calls the right temporal lobe of the brain "the only sensory organ for paranormal reality that we have." Intuition is one of the normal functions of this brain area, continues Dr. Morse, and "the essence of intuition is that there is a direct connection between the human mind and a universal mind."

Bibliography

PART ONE. Even Bad Luck Can Defy the Odds

Bechtel, Stefan, and Roy Stains. *The Good Luck Book*. New York: Workman Publishing, 1997.

Bell, Craig S. *Comprehending Coincidence*. West Chester, Pennyslvania: Chrysalis Books, 2000.

Cousineau, Phil. *Soul Moments: Marvelous Stories of Synchronicity*. Berkeley, California: Conari Press, 1997.

Denning, Hazel M. *Intuition and Synchronicity*. Virginia Beach, Virginia: A.R.E. Press, 2001.

Gwathmey, Emily. *Lots of Luck*. Santa Monica, California: Angel City Press, 1994.

Hopcke, Robert H. *There Are NO Accidents*. New York: Riverhead Books, 1997.

Jung, Carl. *Synchronicity*. Zurich: Rascher Verlag, 1952.

Koestler, Arthur. *The Roots of Coincidence*. London and New York: Vintage Books, 1973.

Konik, Michael. *The Man With the $100,000 Breasts . . . and Other Gambling Stories*. New York: Broadway Books, 1999.

Lears, Jackson. *Something For Nothing: Luck In America*. New York: Viking Press, 2003.

Levinson, Horace C. *Chance, Luck and Statistics*. Mineola, New York: Dover, 1963.

Orkin, Mike. *What Are the Odds?* New York: W.H. Freeman, 2000.

Peat, F. David. *Synchronicity: The Bridge Between Matter and Mind*. New York: Bantam Books, 1987.

Rescher, Nicholas. *Luck: The Brilliant Randomness of Everyday Life*. Pittsburgh: University of Pittsburgh Press, 1995.

Rushnell, Squire. *When God Winks*. New York: Atria Books, 2001.

Scoblete, Frank. *Best Blackjack*. Chicago: Bonus Books, 1996.

Schofield, Phillip, and Peter Hough. *One in A Million*. London: Michael O'Mara Books, 1996.

Vaughan, Alan. *Incredible Coincidence*. New York: Lippincott and Crowell, 1979.

Walsh, James. *True Odds: How Risk Affects Your Everyday Life*. Los Angeles: Silver Lake Publishing, 1998.

Weaver, Warren. *Lady Luck: The Theory of Probability*. New York: Anchor Books, 1963.

Wilson, Robert Anton. *Coincidence*. Scottsdale, Arizona: Falcon Press, 1988.

PART TWO. Premonitions of Good Fortune

Barasch, Marc Ian. *Healing Dreams*. New York: Berkley Publishing, 2000.

Bowles, Norma, and Fran Hynds. *Psi Search*. San Francisco: Harper & Row, 1978.

Broughton, Richard S. *Parapsychology: The Controversial Science*. New York: Ballantine Books, 1992.

Brown, Chip. *Afterwards, You're a Genius*. New York: Riverhead Books, 1999.

Dean, Douglas, and John Mihalasky. *Executive ESP*. Englewood Cliffs, New Jersey: Prentice-Hall, 1974.

Emery, Marcia. *PowerHunch!* Hillsboro, Oregon: Beyond Words, 2001.

Ferguson, Gail. *Cracking the Intuition Code*. Chicago, Illinois: Contemporary Books, 1999.

Gawain, Shakti. *Developing Intuition*. Novato, California: New World Library, 2000.

Gee, Judee. *Intuition: Awakening Your Inner Guide*. York Beach, Maine: Samuel Weiser, 1999.

Gooch, Stan. *The Paranormal*. New York: Harper & Row, 1978.

Grochowski, John. *The Slot Machine Answer Book*. Chicago, Illinois: Bonus Books, 1999.

Hansel, C.E.M. *ESP and Parapsychology*. Buffalo, New York: Prometheus Books, 1980.

Hardy, Alister, Robert Harvie, and Arthur Koestler. *The Challenge of Chance*. New York: Random House, 1974.

Jaegers, Beverly. *The Psychic Paradigm*. New York: Berkley Books, 1998.

Jahn, Robert G., and Brenda J. Dunne. *Margins of Reality*. New York: Harcourt Brace, 1987.

Krippner, Stanley. *Advances in Parapsychological Research*. New York: Plenum Press, 1978.

Loye, David. *The Knowable Future*. New York: John Wiley & Sons, 1978.

Mitchell, Edgar D. *Psychic Exploration*. New York: G. P. Putnam's, 1976.

Moss, Robert. *Conscious Dreaming*. New York: Three Rivers Press, 1996.

Moss, Thelma. *The Probability of the Impossible*. London: Routledge & Kegan Paul, 1976.

Myers, David G. *Intuition: Its Powers and Perils*. New Haven & London: Yale University Press, 2002.

Orloff, Judith. *Second Sight*. New York: Warner Books, 1997.

Radin, Dean. *The Conscious Universe*. New York: HarperCollins, 1997.

Rhine, J. B. *The Reach of the Mind*. New York: William Sloane, 1947.

Rhine, Louisa E. *Mind Over Matter*. New York: Macmillan, 1972.

Robinson, Lynn A. *Divine Intuition*. New York: Dorling Kindersley Publishing, 2001.

Schnabel, Jim. *Remote Viewers: The Secret History of America's Psychic Spies*. New York: Dell Publishing, 1997.

Schulz, Mona Lisa. *Awakening Intuition*. New York: Three Rivers Press, 1998.

Scoblete, Frank. *Best Blackjack*. Chicago: Bonus Books, 1996.

Sinclair, Upton. *Mental Radio*. New York: Macmillan, 1930.

Stone, Hal, and Sidra Stone. *Embracing Our Selves*. Novato, California: Nataraj Publishing, 1989.

Wolman, Benjamin B. *Handbook of Para-Psychology*. New York: Van Nostrand Reinhold, 1977.

PART THREE. Creating Your Own Good Luck

Altman, Donald. *Living Kindness: The Buddha's Ten Guiding Principles For a Blessed Life*. Maui, Hawaii: Inner Ocean, 2003.

Baldwin, Maureen D. *On Winning the Lottery*. Freeport, Illinois: Winners Press, 1998.

Belitz, Charlene, and Meg Lundstrom. *The Power of Flow*. New York: Three Rivers Press, 1998.

Benson, Herbert. *Timeless Healing: The Power and Biology of Belief*. New York: Fireside, 1996.

Day, Laura. *The Circle*. New York: Jeremy P. Tarcher, 2001.

Das, Lama Surya. *Awakening the Buddha Within*. New York: Broadway Books, 1997.

Gunther, Max. *The Luck Factor*. New York: Macmillan, 1973.

Jaffe, Azriela. *Create Your Own Luck*. Avon, Massachusetts: Adams Media, 2000.

Joy, W. Brugh. *Joy's Way*. New York: G. P. Putnam's, 1979.

Morse, Melvin, and Paul Perry. *Where God Lives*. New York: Cliff Street Books, 2000.

Munson, Will. *How Lucky Can You Get?* Englewood, Florida: Eden House, 1990.

Nobles, Aileen. *Divine Abundance*. Malibu, California: Light Transformation Publishing, 2001.

Ponder, Catherine. *The Dynamic Laws of Prosperity*. Englewood Cliffs, New Jersey: Prentice-Hall, 1962.

Rinpoche, Sogyal. *The Tibetan Book of Living and Dying*. New York: HarperCollins, 1993.

Talbot, Michael. *The Holographic Universe*. New York: HarperCollins, 1991.

Temple, Robert K.G. *Netherworld*. London: Arrow Books, 2002.

Thomas, Richard. *It's A Miracle*. New York: Dell, 2002.

Warren, Sharon A. *Magnetizing Your Heart's Desire*. Fountain Hills, Arizona: Amazing Grace Press, 1999.

Wiseman, Richard. *The Luck Factor*. London: Century, 2003.

Zohar, Danah, and Dr. Ian Marshall. *SQ: Spiritual Intelligence*. London and New York: Bloomsbury, 2000.

Index

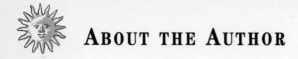

ABOUT THE AUTHOR

Since 1974, when he began his journalism career in Washington, D.C., as an investigative reporter for syndicated columnist Jack Anderson, Randall Fitzgerald has written for a wide variety of publications, including *Reason, Playboy, Alternative Medicine, The Washington Post,* and *The Wall Street Journal.* For twenty years he was a contributing editor for *Reader's Digest,* and he authored or co-authored six previous books on diverse topics. In 1978 he co-founded and co-edited *Second Look*, a magazine devoted to speculative articles about the origins of civilization, the nature of consciousness, and the search for other life in the universe. He has been interviewed on several hundred radio and television programs concerning his books and magazine articles, including appearances on NBC's *Today*, ABC's *20/20*, C-Span, and CNN.